The Mercedes-Benz MIDIbus

Front Cover Photograph: Mercedes-Benz midibuses were not all the same, by a long way. With a dozen or more coachbuilders involved in their production, there was a lot of variety. Two contrasting styles with Streamline of Bath are shown here, on The Centre in Bristol, while their drivers exchange views. On the left, K691 UFV is a 709D, with Plaxton Beaver 23-seat body, while on the right, M48 BEG is an 811D, with 31-seat Marshall bodywork. Marshall was one of the majority of coachbuilders who incorporated the standard Mercedes-Benz windscreen into their design, but Plaxton used a wider screen. The photograph was taken on the special VE Day Bank Holiday Monday, 8 May 1995. Both buses, bought new by Streamline, are working services that were lightly-used on Sundays and Bank Holidays, so were funded by Avon County Council. The 544 was a version of the weekday Bristol CityLine double-deck route 44, while the 649's equivalent, out to the dormitory town of Keynsham, was the Badgerline 349 and Abus A49. *Lee Turton.*

Rear cover photographs.

Rear cover, top: The Mercedes-Benz midibus was perfectly suited to both urban and rural work and routes do not come much more rural than this, Stagecoach Cumberland's 77, 'The Honister Rambler'. The bus, also numbered 77 (K877 GHH), is a 709D with Alexander (Belfast) 25-seat bodywork. It is seen at the top of the Honister Pass, at 1,170ft (356m) above sea-level, having faced a gradient of 1-in-4 (25 per cent) on the way. The special livery for this Lake District service was derived from some open-top double-deckers transferred from Southdown, where this apple-green and cream had been re-adopted before Stagecoach took control.

Rear cover, middle: With the Mendip Hills behind it, First Somerset & Avon 51079 (L879 VHT) has just called in at the village of Wookey, famous for the Wookey Hole Caves, on its way between England's smallest city, Wells, and the coast at Burnham-on-Sea. 51079 is a 709D, with Plaxton Beaver 23-seat bodywork.

Rear cover, bottom: In the beautiful Cotswold village of Bibury in Gloucestershire, Cotswold Green's N951 NAP passes in front of the creeper-clad Swan Hotel, on the infrequent council-funded service from/to Cirencester. This 709D, with Alexander Sprint bodywork, was new to Stagecoach East Kent.

The Title Page photograph: The Mercedes-Benz midibus was at its most active several years after the 1986 deregulation of bus services, by which time second-hand examples were becoming available to small independent operators, many of whom were competing against incumbent major operators. This is a 2001 scene, in Dorchester Street, Bath. The leading bus is Bath Bus Company's J611 WHJ, which has worked into the city from the southern suburbs on service S2. The bus is an 811D, new to County Bus & Coach of Harlow, Essex, with a Plaxton Beaver body of London-style, wide-doorway, 28-seat configuration. Latterly in Arriva ownership, it has been repainted using the Arriva colour boundaries, while the bus behind, still in full Arriva livery, is owned by Faresaver of Chippenham. This bus, H204 EKO, is on the 231 between the two centres, which also competes with First. It is a 709D, with Carlyle 25-seat body. It was new to Maidstone & District, which was later acquired by Arriva. After Faresaver, this bus went on to serve two other small operators in the Bristol area and is illustrated again in Section 3.

The Mercedes-Benz MIDIbus

Allan Macfarlane

First published in Great Britain in 2023 by
Pen and Sword Transport
An imprint of
Pen & Sword Books Ltd
Yorkshire - Philadelphia

Copyright © Allan Macfarlane, 2023

ISBN 978 1 39902 353 5

The right of Allan Macfarlane to be identified as Author of this work has been asserted by him in accordance with the Copyright, Designs and Patents Act 1988.

A CIP catalogue record for this book is available from the British Library.

All rights reserved. No part of this book may be reproduced or transmitted in any form or by any means, electronic or mechanical including photocopying, recording or by any information storage and retrieval system, without permission from the Publisher in writing.

Typeset in 11/14 Palatino
Typeset by SJmagic DESIGN SERVICES, India.

Printed and bound by Printworks Global Ltd, London/Hong Kong.

Pen & Sword Books Ltd incorporates the Imprints of Pen & Sword Books Archaeology, Atlas, Aviation, Battleground, Discovery, Family History, History, Maritime, Military, Naval, Politics, Railways, Select, Transport, True Crime, Fiction, Frontline Books, Leo Cooper, Praetorian Press, Seaforth Publishing, Wharncliffe and White Owl.

For a complete list of Pen & Sword titles please contact

PEN & SWORD BOOKS LIMITED
George House, Units 12 & 13, Beevor Street, Off Pontefract Road,
Barnsley, South Yorkshire, S71 1HN, England
E-mail: enquiries@pen-and-sword.co.uk
Website: www.pen-and-sword.co.uk

or

PEN AND SWORD BOOKS
1950 Lawrence Rd, Havertown, PA 19083, USA
E-mail: Uspen-and-sword@casematepublishers.com
Website: www.penandswordbooks.com

CONTENTS

Preface		6
Section 1	Design and Market Forces	8
Section 2	The Ins and Outs	73
Section 3	The Mercedes-Benz Midibus in South West England	89
FirstBus	The National fleet re-numbering scheme of January 2004: An outline of the renumbering of Mercedes midibuses in south-west England	172
Scale Model Mercedes-Benz Midibuses		176

PREFACE

I have always lived in the Bristol area where, famously, the region's buses when I was young were both owned by and built by the operator, Bristol Tramways & Carriage Company (BT&CC). As I met other enthusiasts as a teenager, my knowledge of Bristol buses and the company grew rapidly. I soon made acquaintances with staff at the two successors to the BT&CC, Bristol Omnibus Company Ltd, the operator, and Bristol Commercial Vehicles Ltd, the chassis-builder.

I began to study the design, development and history of Bristol chassis and of Bristol coachwork. For a time in the 1960s, I worked in the sales office at Bristol Commercial Vehicles, so gained first-hand knowledge of chassis design and production. I began to write articles for the enthusiasts' magazine, *Buses Illustrated*, and I later turned to writing books about Bristols. I also revived the enthusiasts' society The Bristol Interest Circle, for which I produced the club magazine for 34 years.

With both Bristol and their partner Eastern Coach Works of Lowestoft being closed down in the turmoil that was the 1980s (as explained in more detail in this book), I was well aware of what was succeeding them – hordes of Ford Transit *minibuses*. Like many enthusiasts, I met their arrival with very little enthusiasm, yet they did help to boost travel by public transport and, as they were still part of the ongoing activities of the Bristol Omnibus Company and its neighbours, I dutifully recorded them.

I admit I still did not take a great deal of notice when the Mercedes-Benz midibus came on to the scene in the late 1980s (initially, there were few locally). That changed when Jim Whiting of Capital Transport publications asked me to compile the 1995 edition of his *South West Buses* illustrated fleet-list book. By this time, many operators in the south-west had turned to the Mercedes-Benz midibus for fleet renewal and compiling the fleet-lists for the book made me realise what amazing variety there was in the marque. The different specifications of chassis and the wide range of makes and styles of bodywork became very apparent. I obtained publicity brochures, from which I learned about the mechanical differences and what materials were used in bodywork construction. Here was a small bus that had every bit as much variety as a big bus. Importantly, it was carrying out a vital role in providing public transport very efficiently and also it had created a lot of jobs with small British bodywork manufacturers. The marque gained considerable respect from operators and its importance should not be underestimated.

To the critics of small buses I would say, was the midibus really that small? When I was a boy, the standard single-decker which we knew and loved, such as the Bristol L, AEC Regal or Leyland Tiger, was only 8.4 metres long and had no more than 35 seats – data closely matched by the Mercedes-Benz 811D/814D.

I am grateful to several people from the bus industry who have gladly passed on information about operating or manufacturing Merc midibuses, as well as those who were able to fill the gaps in my own photography for this book. My thanks go to Ken Baker, Martin Curtis, Nigel Eadon-Clarke, Graham Jones, Robin Orbell, Dave Russell & Deric Pemberton, Paul Savage, John Seale, Dr Mike Walker and John Young, and to others who have shared information with me. A great deal of data was obtained from the newssheets and fleet-lists published by The PSV Circle and the online database of buslistsontheweb.co.uk. Other sources include *BUSES* magazine, the British Bus Publishing series of Bus Handbooks and, of course, the

The author is seen here at the wheel of one of Buglers Coaches' Mercedes-Benz midibuses that incorporated a wheel-chair lift at the back, for working dial-a-ride services under contract to Avon County Council. The bus is a Marshall-bodied 711D, M845 CWS. Bugler's two earlier Mercs were short wheelbase 811Ds, bodied by Robin Hood, F432 OBK, with a tail-lift, and F251 OPX, fully seated with 29 coach seats.

Internet, which also provided access to archived trade magazine data.

I do have experience of driving Mercs. After taking early retirement in 1995, long term friend Alan Peters, who ran Abus in Bristol, suggested I obtained a PSV driving licence. This I obtained through the driving school of Bugler's Coaches. Having passed, Bob Bugler immediately offered me holiday cover on one of the regular dial-a-ride services he provided, on contract to Bristol City Council. This resulted in me driving each of his three Mercedes-Benz midibuses, two of which incorporated a tail-lift for passengers in wheelchairs.

I later joined the driving staff at Abus, or with the associated business of Simon Munden's Crown Coaches. Most of this time was spent driving double-deckers – Bristols, usually – but in time, Abus added a Mercedes-Benz Vario to stock, as a back-up for their Optare Solos. I had just the occasional job driving this bus.

In the following account, reference to the seating layout of the bodywork mounted on Mercedes-Benz chassis is stated in the widely accepted standard format, so that B25F indicates that the vehicle is fitted with bus seats for 25 passengers and that the doorway is at the front. C33F means that coach seats are installed for 33 persons. The other term is DP, which shows that the seats are of coach-type comfort, but the vehicle is equally suitable for both coach and bus work – i.e., it has a Dual Purpose.

All the photographs in this book are of my own taking, unless otherwise acknowledged.

Allan Macfarlane,
Westbury-on-Trym, Bristol,
June 2022

SECTION 1
DESIGN AND MARKET FORCES

MIDIBUS … OR **MINI**BUS?
What is the difference between a *mini*bus and a *midi*bus? The enthusiasts' vehicle-recording organisation The PSV Circle defined a minibus as containing up to 16 seats and principally dedicated to welfare duties or as a personnel carrier. Vehicles of a similar capacity were certainly also used for passenger carrying on public bus routes and, even with seating for 20 or 21, they would still fit people's ideas of a minibus when compared with the full-sized buses of the day. To comply with stringent regulations for Public Service Vehicles (PSVs – subsequently called Passenger Carrying Vehicles or PCVs), internal headroom, seat width and spacing, gangway width and passenger-door dimensions had to meet certain criteria.

There had long been a demand for the occasional minibus to cover, for example, a special low-usage service over restricted roads, whether in isolated country regions of Britain, or in ancient city centres. Suitable medium-sized panel vans would be converted into minibuses to cater for the need. The launch in 1965 of Ford's Transit made available a very suitable van which could be modified to minibus status. The factory-made Transit panel-van was used at first, though for PSV work, a high roof would be required. After the Transit was made available as a chassis-cowl (i.e., with just with the bonnet and front end fitted, but no other bodywork), specialist van bodybuilders produced what were called parcel vans and, being taller and often wider, these lent themselves admirably to conversion to full PSV status. Bedford responded with their CF in chassis-cowl form, as did Freight-Rover with their Sherpa. From what were regarded at the time as 'foreign' makers (rather disparagingly), only a small number of minibuses were produced. An example was Germany's Mercedes-Benz L508D factory-produced van, which could readily be converted into a minibus, with seating for up to 20 passengers.

THE 'MINIBUS REVOLUTION'
In the spring of 1984, something of a revolution in British bus provision began, when Devon General started to put into practice a radical idea of running a network of services within the city of Exeter with 16-seat minibuses working at a high frequency – every 3 to 5 minutes, maybe. These were in place of conventional buses, even 74-seat double-deckers, that had run every 15 to 30 minutes. The minibuses were Ford Transits, with parcel van bodywork built by the well-known firm of Dormobile, but converted into minibuses by several other, mainly small, bodybuilders.

The public was won over quickly. Intending passengers simply walked to their nearest bus-stop and within minutes, a bus was there to take them on their way … albeit a perhaps noisy and sometimes cramped bus, which tended to lean and roll alarmingly while negotiating residential roads.

The idea, for all that, spread rapidly, particularly among the bus operators that, like Devon General, were under the wing of the state-owned National Bus Company (NBC). Even in big cities like Bristol, 16-seat Transits started to become very numerous. A major disadvantage in the big cities, though, was that the journeys could be long, so that in busy periods, the minibuses, even though frequent, could be packed with standing passengers. Because of their narrow width, there was insufficient space in the

The minibus 'craze' began in Exeter in 1984, when Devon General quickly turned the city's bus services over to frequent minibus operation, with 16-seat Ford Transits. Three are seen here, but many hundreds of similar minibuses followed suit throughout the country.

gangway for those at the back of the bus to reach the front door with ease, resulting in a trend to 'escape' through the emergency exit in the middle of the rear wall of the bus. This, of course, was not recommended, nor was it safe, and most certainly it was not legally permissible.

Another boost to making the minibus a popular choice was that Britain's bus services were due to be deregulated as from 26 October 1986 and operators knew an answer to the expected free-for-all was to have wall-to-wall coverage with minibuses, leaving no room for competitors. Minibuses were fairly inexpensive to buy and run – even their drivers tended to be employed on a lower rate of pay.

The start of the fashion for large quantities of minibuses occurred in 1985 at an opportune moment. Ford had developed an all-new Transit, the so-called Mark III or VE6, identified by its sloping front instead of level bonnet. Ford was therefore eager to shift the remaining Mark II Transits from their production lines and holding sites. The NBC spoke for a large number and probably obtained them on favourable terms. After conversion of their parcel van bodies to 16-seat minibuses, they entered service with B- and C-prefix registration numbers, though a few Mark IIs remained to receive D-prefix number-plates after August 1986.

As it happened, a similar new-model launch was about to occur in Germany. Mercedes-Benz had developed a successor to their medium van, so the NBC spoke for most of the remaining

DESIGN AND MARKET FORCES • 9

production of right-hand-drive L608D vans, for conversion to 20-seat minibuses.

THE DEVELOPMENT OF THE MERCEDES-BENZ VAN

Until the mid-1950s, Mercedes-Benz built luxury cars or a range of lorries and coaches. Mercedes-Benz did not do vans. That sector of the market was left to their compatriots, such as Hanomag, Henschel, Opel, Tempo, Volkswagen and even DKW. Only in 1955 did Mercedes-Benz enter this market. Their offering was coded L319 (L for *Lastwagen*, i.e., truck) and was designed for a laden weight of 3.6 tonnes, being powered by a 43bhp 4-cylinder diesel engine. Mercedes also offered the vehicle as a minibus, coded O319, the 'O' signifying a factory-produced 'Omnibus'. Up to 18 seats could be installed, but with no gangway and dependent on several doorways being located along the side. From 1963, a new style of identification code was applied, which became popular with several commercial vehicle manufacturers. Divided into two parts, the first single- or double-figure of the code expressed the maximum permitted gross vehicle weight (gvw) to the nearest full tonne, while the final two figures indicated the engine's output, but shown as 1/10th of the bhp rating, again rounded up or down. So, the Mercedes 3.6 tonne van, now with a 50bhp, Diesel, engine became the L405D. (The digits when attached to the front door for model identification excluded the L.)

THE DÜSSELDORF VAN

A new style of van replaced the derivatives of the L319 and O319 from 1967. This was distinguished by a short, sloping bonnet, to house the front end of the engine, as by now the flat-fronted, engine-within-cab layout had become undesirable, for maintenance and safety reasons. The van's windscreen was deep and gently curved, with square corners, yet it was made to appear wrap-round because it was separated by just a thin dividing strip from the flat side-glasses. These

The Mercedes-Benz O319 had quite a following in Éire. FYI 794, with Frank McConnell of Cavan, does not have the multiple side doors, but does have glazing in the roof's cant panels.

narrow side glasses, or quarter-lights, met the vertical cab-door pillars.

The new van was built at Mercedes-Benz's factory in Düsseldorf and became known as the Düsseldorf Transporter Type 2, or T2, although this designation was not widely used. Gross weights, reflected in the model codes again, ranged from approximately 3 tonnes up to 6 tonnes, with engine output at about 60-70bhp. The dimensions and load-capacity of the new L507D permitted a respectable minibus to be created in the UK. On the Continent, however,

Right: This factory-produced Omnibus version of the Mercedes-Benz 'Düsseldorf' van, coded O613D, is seen with a French operator. It is notably wider than the vans that were supplied to the UK for minibus conversion.

Below: Typical of several hundred Mercedes-Benz L608D *mini*buses put to work in the UK around 1984-86 is Western National's 130 (C981 GCV). The 20-seat PSV conversion was carried out by PMT Engineering at Stoke-on-Trent, but it has a lamentably inadequate destination screen. In this bus, there is still a solid panel aft of the door, yet other converters, as shown by the bus in the background, placed a window here.

Düsseldorf offered factory-produced Omnibus versions, with wider bodies and more power, such as the O613D. Upgrading of the range over the years saw the emergence of the L508D and L608D and it was the L608D that became the target of the NBC's buying spree in the mid-1980s, most receiving C- or D-prefix registrations.

INTRODUCING THE T1 …

Another new family of van had started to emerge from 1977 and was referred to as the 'Transporter 1', or 'T1'. It initially comprised the 207D and 307D, for 2.5 to 3.5 tonnes gvw, these being joined later by the 407D, while the approximately 70bhp engine was upgraded to around 80bhp before, finally, a 100bhp engine was offered in the 410D. Built at Bremen, the T1 replaced the lighter versions of the Düsseldorf vans, the L307D and L407D. The T1 was occasionally used in the UK as the basis for small minibuses.

… AND THE GROUND-BREAKING T2

It was not until 1986 that the L508D and L608D were replaced. The new Düsseldorf van was again known as the 'T2', though this time the moniker gained wide acceptance and it is this application of the term T2 that is used in this book. The full-width bonnet was short and downward sloping, as on the earlier Düsseldorf vans, and the T1, while the vehicle continued to feature a large, curved windscreen, though now very gently dipping at its centre. It again had a full-width black grille, with rectangular headlights at either side. As with the T1, the flashing direction indicators were now on the corners, alongside the headlights. The general impression from the front of the T2 Mercedes-Benz was very easy on the eye and, actually, it almost gave a smiling appearance.

The T2 catered for a range of weights and powers that extended beyond those of its predecessor. The starting point, and to directly

The Bremen-built T1 Mercedes van was only occasionally used for minibus applications. This 16-seat 407D of 1989, F478 PAE, was operated by Arrow on a contracted service in the Bristol suburbs. Converters Made-to-Measure of Stockport had installed a full-height door in the side, while other businesses merely adapted the nearside cab door.

replace the L508D and L608D, were the 507D (the code still signifying around 5 tonnes, but with about 70bhp now) and the 609D. These new vans were joined by two stronger and/or more powerful versions, the 709D and the 811D.

The launch of the T2, however, was rather too late to benefit from the minibus boom in Britain, as the NBC in particular had gorged itself on 'stock-clearance' L608Ds and Mark II Ford Transits. The T2 did come into its own before long, however, when the first-generation minibuses were selected for replacement by something a little larger, with a bit more space. It must be recorded, though, that the Ford Transits had been remarkably robust; they simply had too low a capacity – a consequence of the boost these buses had given to local travel.

After bus services had been deregulated in October 1986, many small private operators began bus work, this mainly coming after winning competitive tenders for council funding for running unremunerative routes. Many of the operators started these services with ex-NBC Transits and the like, as the income from these services could not justify the expenditure on a new vehicle. Some contracts, however, did specify the use of a new vehicle and a Mercedes T2 was often the type chosen. It was only a matter of time before used T2s made their way into small operators' fleets.

THE T2 AS A BUS

The Mercedes-Benz 507D found little custom as a PSV, as its specification dictated that only 16 seats could be accommodated – the same as in a Ford Transit, Freight-Rover Sherpa or Bedford CF, but in a more expensive vehicle. Besides, used versions of the other makes were becoming available already. For a new bus, it was the 609D that appealed to PSV operators initially.

E930 YAM is a rare variant of the Mercedes-Benz T2, being a 507D. Note the small wheels. It was converted from a van to a 16-seat minibus by Reeve-Burgess, using their distinctive destination box outline. Clapton Coaches of Clapton, near Bath, were working it on an Avon County Council funded rural service, between Midsomer Norton and Bristol, via Timsbury.

The basic van body shell could be fitted out as a 20-seater bus (with single seats on one side), or with 24 coach seats, where a narrower gangway was permitted. The 709D van came into the same categories, while a few high-quality coach conversions were made from 811D van shells.

The first major consignment of T2 minibuses to take to the streets comprised twenty van-conversion 709Ds, which went to work in the Tyne & Wear area from January 1987, for Busways Travel Services (numbers 1401-1420: D401-420 TFT).

In May 1987, *Commercial Motor* magazine carried a report about the business that had converted those Busways 709D vans to PSV status. This was **Reeve Burgess** of Pilsley, near Chesterfield, a subsidiary of the Plaxton Group plc, Britain's leading coach body-builder. An important inclusion in the report, though, was the announcement by Reeve Burgess that they had prepared a *coach-built*, steel-framed body, incorporating a steel subframe, which was being mounted on a bare 609D *chassis-cowl*. This was a different kind of Merc – *in no way was this a van!*

The new Reeve Burgess coach-built body was to be called the 'Beaver' and would be somewhat wider than the van-conversion, approaching 2,300mm. It was therefore capable of holding regulation-width (850mm) double seats, placed either side of a conventional 500mm-wide gangway. Now, 25 passengers could be seated. The quoted price with coach seats was £28,340; a 25-seat bus version, fitted with a base-tray for fare-collection equipment and a bulkhead behind the driver, plus extra hand-rails, and intended for the 709D chassis-cowl, was being finalised and would cost £29,400. The prototype 609D/Beaver coach was duly supplied in June 1987 to Chambers of Stevenage. It was handled by a dealer who registered the coach as D638 KMM;

An historic vehicle, as D638 KMM, a 609D, has the prototype Reeve-Burgess 'Beaver' body. It is believed to have been the only coach-built Mercedes-Benz with a D-prefix registration. It was supplied to Chambers of Stevenage in June 1987. Despite having coach seats, it is seen on local bus work. Note the wide windscreen, the shape of which is cleverly mirrored by the destination box glazing. *Transport Nostalgia*

it is believed to be the *only* D-registered Merc with *coachbuilt* PSV bodywork. It ran in a white livery, with red top to the roof and a shallow red skirt, plus a narrow blue band around the middle. It carried a Reeve-Burgess badge on the front of the bonnet, above the offside headlight, which was possibly unique.

As a matter of fact, Reeve-Burgess had been producing coach-built bodies for some years, but on other makes of chassis-cowl. After some very plain 'Reebur' bodies had been mounted on Ford Transit and Bedford CF chassis, Reeve Burgess bodied several Dodge 50-series chassis-cowls (later examples badged as Renaults) and these bodies were attractive and well-styled. Popular with council welfare departments, the biggest fleets of PSV versions went to Plymouth CityBus and South Yorkshire Transport around the time of deregulation in late 1986, so also had D-prefix registrations. Subsequently, the Beaver body was made available for the Renault-Dodge 50-series, as well as for the Iveco 49-10.

Although the Mercedes T2 chassis-cowl was supplied with the entire windscreen attached (the same item as used in the van and also in the larger, forward-control range of Mercedes-Benz LN2 lorries), Reeve-Burgess dispensed with this for their Beaver, choosing to install a wider windscreen to suit the wider coach-built body. This helped to distinguish the Beaver from most other midibus bodies that followed. The new windscreen's pillars, together with the deep quarter-lights, would be more-or-less flush with the side panelling ahead of the doorway. The Reeve-Burgess screen still featured the gentle dip in the centre at the bottom. It had rounded lower corners, but at the top, the corners were square.

The destination screen initially incorporated into the Beaver body was a shallow affair, level with the roof, but the glazing was to the full width of the bus. Cleverly, this glass mirrored the shape of the windscreen below it, by having square lower corners and rounded upper corners. This was a distinctive and attractive feature, and it was also incorporated into Reeve-Burgess T2 van conversions, which made those vehicles easily recognizable. Before long, though, there was a call for clearer and deeper destination screens, incorporating larger route numbers and, in keeping with full-sized buses, using standard-format blinds that were deep enough to include via points. The top of the box in the Beaver was therefore raised, with a gentle slope behind it down to the roof, while having a more upright face. It was, though, a little narrower than before, although the glass still mirrored the shape of the windscreen. The original shallow and wide box remained an option for a while. Subsequent coach versions of the Beaver still carried a shallow box, but the glass became a little narrower, with simple rounded ends. The glass usually only carried the owner's name, anyway.

The Reeve-Burgess Beaver featured large, square-cornered side windows, reaching quite high on the sides for the benefit of standing passengers, while there was a ridge along the cove panels above them. Tipper ventilators were available for the full-sized windows. The Beaver was a well-balanced and very attractive design.

MINIBUS ... OR MIDIBUS?

With a 25-seat capability, the Reeve-Burgess Beaver was by no means a minibus – it was a midibus. Should there be any doubt that it was a midibus, the publicity brochures issued for the range by Mercedes-Benz (UK) Ltd were entitled *Mercedes-Benz chassis-cowls for midibus bodies*.

THE INITIAL T2 SPECIFICATION

This work will ignore the 507D variant because, being on the small side and never more than a minibus in the popular interpretation of the word, it was seldom chosen for PSV work. The model did not remain listed very long in any case, though long enough to be uprated to 508D status. Otherwise, the T2 was powered by the Mercedes-Benz OM364-family engine, a 3.97-litre, 4-cylinder unit, with bore and stroke of 97.5mm by 133mm. The basic engine in naturally-aspirated form could produce 86-90bhp at up to 2,800rpm and was used in the 609D and 709D. A turbocharged version of the engine was produced, designated

OM364A; in this, the powerful ejection of exhaust gas was used to turn a turbine, this in turn boosting the injection of fuel into the cylinders, the result being an increase of power to 115bhp at 2,600rpm; it was this unit that was used in the 811D.

Transmission options were a Mercedes-Benz 5-speed manual gearbox, with direct-drive to 5th gear, or either a Mercedes-Benz or an Alison 4-speed automatic box. T2s with automatic boxes tended to develop a distinguishing whistle while accelerating. A maximum top speed of 72mph was quoted by the makers, depending on the engine and the rear-axle ratio.

The wheelbase of the T2 was 4,250mm. The overall length for the chassis-cowl was 6,940mm, while the complete panel van was 7,210mm. Front overhang was 820mm. At the rear, the overhang for a bare chassis was 1,870mm, while on a completed van shell it was 2,140mm. On coach-built bodywork it was normally around 2,000mm, producing an overall length of approximately 7,000mm. The overall width of the base van was 2,192mm, but a coach-built body on the chassis-cowl would be around 2,300mm wide, to allow a familiar bus-like interior. The chassis was rear-wheel-drive, with disc brakes on the front wheels and drums on the rear, using hydraulic actuation on the 609D and 709D, but an air/hydraulic system on the 811D. An exhaust brake was a standard fitting. The chassis had a turning circle of 15m, with power-assistance fitted to the steering as standard.

The chassis frame was a simple ladder layout, just gently cranked over the rear axle. On chassis-cowls for PSV work, components were kept clear of the area behind the front nearside wheel, to provide space for the entrance doorway and steps.

THE *BAUMUSTER*

An interesting point that should be noted concerns the complete chassis-number, or Vehicle Identity Number (VIN), of a Mercedes-Benz commercial vehicle. It commences with the letters WDB, which is the World Manufacturer Identifier, in which W indicates Germany and DB refers to Daimler-Benz, the name quoted on the earlier chassis plates. There then follows a six-figure code. This is called a *Baumuster*, which translates as a build or specification number.

It may not be fully appreciated by vehicle recorders that each of these six-figure *Baumusters* is exclusive to each chassis model code. The first three figures relate to the vehicle's gross tonnage and the second three to the engine power. The *Baumusters* used for T2 chassis-cowls for PSV bodywork were: 668003 for the 609D; 669003 for the 709D; and 670303 for the 811D. The *Baumuster* for van shells for PSV conversion differed slightly – the 609D, 709D and 811D vans were 668063, 669063 and 670363, respectively.

Within the VIN, the *Baumuster* was followed by the digits 20, which had an internal significance, yet also referred to the product being right-hand-drive. It is a well-known fact that the individual numbers for Mercedes-Benz chassis were not exactly sequential, but were applied in a slightly random fashion, believed to be a means to counter fraud.

The prototype Reeve Burgess Beaver-bodied 609D, D638 KMM, had the VIN of WDB668003-20-798763. After nearing the end of the -20-980000 range in 1990, the series changed to -2P-, but that was abandoned in 1992 in favour of a -2N- series. In practice, although vehicle records usually show the hyphens, the chassis plates on the vehicles excluded them. Furthermore, it should be noted that, very occasionally, chassis plates were stamped with incorrect figures.

DON'T CALL IT A VAN!

It is important to stress that a T2 van shell supplied for PSV conversion incorporated several differences from the van that was sold for goods carrying and industrial work. Many items were changed to assist in meeting British and Irish PSV standards. Most importantly, there was a glazed emergency door on the off-side, near the back of the body. In addition, instead of double rear doors, there was a large, single-piece rear window, with a luggage boot below that. There was an upgraded suspension system, using parabolic front springs and conventional leaf rear springs, although this was still criticised as giving a van-like ride – from which one can only assume the critics spent some time riding in vans. It also had specially chosen gear ratios. Conversely, items useful in a cargo-carrying van were excluded. The amount of work that British bodybuilding firms put into the completion of these van shells to achieve PSV certification should not be underestimated.

EARLY DEVELOPMENTS

The idea of building bodywork on to the T2 chassis-cowl was soon taken up by other bodybuilders. In Leeds, **Optare** had grander ideas. This firm had only been formed in 1985, to carry on the coachbuilding activities formerly known as Charles H. Roe. British-Leyland, Roe's owner, had wanted to close the plant, a decision brought on by a worrying drop in orders for double-deck buses; this was a major result of the Government's plan to deregulate bus services and to sell off NBC subsidiaries to the private sector – nobody knew what would be happening after 'Deregulation Day' on 26 October 1986, so were not willing to invest in new buses. Furthermore, by 1984 interest in minibuses was beginning to develop rapidly, to the detriment of double-decker manufacturing. A Roe director, Russell Richardson, bid to save the factory – and several employees' jobs – and so was formed Optare (Latin for 'to choose'). Initially, some Roe-style bodies continued to be produced, but quickly new markets were explored. Optare and the enterprising Russell Richardson saw the midibus market as worthy of a specially-made vehicle, rather than a modified van. They came up with the Optare 'CityPacer', a 25-seater with a very stylish swept-back frontal profile, containing a very deep and gently curved windscreen. The chassis Optare had chosen on which to build the CityPacer was that of a 5.5 tonne gross Volkswagen LT55 van. At the same time, Metropolitan-Cammell Weymann (MCW), the Midlands-based bus and train carriage builder, was launching their 'Metrorider', an integral 25-seater with Cummins engine, yet of similar outline, even if less eye-catching.

The availability of a Mercedes-Benz chassis-cowl was seen by Optare as a way to extend the CityPacer theme to fill or even create a niche

Optare of Leeds, soon after its formation out of the old-established Charles H. Roe coachbuilding business, started exploring new markets, with purpose-built midibuses. The Optare CityPacer was a stylish 25-seater, based on a Volkswagen chassis. This demonstrator, D81 NWW, is seen while working for South Midland, in Wantage.

In the same category as the Optare CityPacer was the integral MCW Metrorider. F111 YWO was supplied in 1988 to Rhymney Valley District Council's Inter Valley Link operation.

market. Optare saw that a longer version of the Mercedes T2 could produce a bus or coach with up to 33 seats. There was nothing else on offer in that sphere to match the handling, accessibility and running costs of a Merc. The only alternatives were short versions of full-sized, heavier duty PSVs, calculated to cost rather a lot in relation to their earning capacity when compared to a Merc.

The problem was how to produce a longer version of the T2 chassis to accommodate the 33-seat body, which was to be as much as 1,400mm longer than standard, at 8,400mm (or 27 feet 6 inches, which had been the maximum length of a conventional single-deck bus before 1950). Mercedes-Benz only offered the one frame, with the wheelbase of 4,250mm. Discussions between Optare and Mercedes concluded that a wheelbase of 4,800mm would be suitable for the longer bus but Mercedes would not be able to produce a long wheelbase version without upsetting their automated production techniques for what may only be a small quantity. It is understood that conventional 4,250mm chassis would be supplied and Optare would oversee getting the extension carried out in the UK, clearly to the standards Mercedes-Benz demanded. In order to cater for the additional weight, the model to be supplied to Optare would be the 811D.

Optare apparently decided to contract out the job of extending the chassis, including the propshaft, pipes and cabling, by the necessary 550mm. Optare then launched the model as an Optare product, in keeping with their ethos, calling it the Optare 'StarRider'. Of note was that neither the Mercedes-Benz windscreen, nor even the front cowl, was used by Optare, the StarRider having a home-designed, continuously-sloping front-end, formed from glass-reinforced-plastic (GRP) and incorporating a lifting bonnet for daily engine checks. There was not even a decorative grille, but the Mercedes-Benz three-pointed star badge was carried between the headlamps. Body construction utilised all-welded, tubular steel framework, which was panelled in aluminium, while using GRP for areas susceptible to receiving damage. Prices for the StarRider were quoted as starting at £37,500.

The first StarRiders entered service in August 1987, at the start of E-prefix registrations. Some of the first built went to one of Optare's local major bus operators, the West Yorkshire Passenger Transport Executive (2001-4: E201-4 PWY), for use on a Bradford 'Shop Hopper' service – a role more in keeping with minibus usage. No fewer than 24 StarRiders were then delivered to one of the first NBC operators to be privatised and to develop its own vehicle buying policy, namely Badgerline Ltd of Weston-super-Mare, North Somerset (3800-3823: E800-823 MOU).

All went well until some teething problems developed. To hasten the return of some StarRiders to service if three or four were off the road, some good parts from faulty buses were transferred to replace failed items in others – a common practice. However, it was found in these circumstances that prop-shafts did not always fit perfectly. It is understood that the different engineering firms that had lengthened the chassis had not adopted precise, standardised measurements. Optare unfortunately had rather a lot of warrantee work to undertake, during which time StarRiders built for stock, or to act as demonstrators, were loaned out as cover. But the problems were soon overcome and the StarRider attracted several orders, vindicating Optare's decision to go for a long wheelbase 33-seater.

The Optare StarRider broke new ground by initiating a long wheelbase version of the Mercedes-Benz chassis, to achieve a capacity of 33 seats – equal to more than *two minibuses*. F369 BUA is one of several StarRider demonstrators and is seen here in Bristol, on loan to Badgerline.

Despite the probable temptation, Optare and Mercedes-Benz had not entered into an exclusivity deal regarding the long wheelbase version of the chassis. As soon as practicable, therefore, Mercedes included the long wheelbase 811D chassis-cowl into their production line for the UK and Éire and, indeed, most later chassis to the 811D PSV specification were built to this length. The turning-circle with the longer wheelbase was increased from 15m to nearly 17m.

In 1990, Optare built, for assessment, a StarRider body mounted behind a conventional Mercedes-Benz cowl and windscreen. Designated the SRE, it was said to save £1,000 on the price of the familiar StarRider. It did not go into production.

A MAINSTREAM BODYBUILDER JOINS IN

The next bodybuilder to turn to constructing separate bodies for the T2 chassis-cowl was **Walter Alexander Ltd** of Falkirk. Alexander was a very long established coachbuilder of full-sized buses, and its products were well known and often very stylish. Being based in Stirlingshire, its principal customers had always been Scottish and only since the late 1950s had English and Welsh customers spoken for Alexander bodywork in sizeable numbers. In the mid-1980s, Alexander decided to take advantage of the minibus boom and turned its hand to converting Ford Transit parcel vans and Mercedes-Benz L608Ds, not only at Falkirk but at their acquired production facility at Mallusk, near Belfast. They progressed to designing a separate body for the Merc T2. This was of all-aluminium construction, as now used in their full-sized bodywork. Both the framework and the principal panelling were in aluminium.

The prototype body was built on a 709D chassis and contained 25 seats. It was registered in November 1987 through the Stirling Vehicle Licensing Office (VLO) as E40 OMS. It was aimed at demonstration purposes, for which it carried a large Alexander name on the sides, in the style of the coachbuilder's emblem. The side windows, although deep, were mounted rather high in the body, producing shallow cove-panels. Unlike concurrent full-sized Alexander bodies, these windows featured square corners. The driver was provided with his/her own door on the offside.

The product soon attracted custom, and the first production body was a 25-seat 709D bus that entered service with Burnley & Pendle Transport in February 1988 (91: E91 LBV); it was soon followed by three more (92-94: E92-94 LHG). Unlike E40 OMS, these bodies had round-cornered side windows, although square-cornered glazing was still available initially. Chesterfield Borough Transport took nine more or less identical buses around the same time, as numbers 90-98 (E90-98 YWB), with Spire Sprinter branding. Other bodies from the same batch were supplied to small operators in central Scotland, while at the same time a batch was shared by two English subsidiaries of the Scottish-based Stagecoach Group, namely Cumberland Motor Services and United Counties Omnibus Company of Northampton. Before long, the Alexander-bodied 709D became one of the Stagecoach Group's standard buses and appeared in large numbers all over Great Britain.

The body-numbers perpetuated the AM (Aluminium Minibus) series that had been applied to the van conversions, but then the name Alexander 'Sprint' was coined to accompany the Alexander 'Dash' body for the Dennis Dart lightweight, rear-engined single-decker, all inferring that these small buses were livelier than the seemingly pedestrian conventional buses.

As with the Reeve Burgess Beaver, early Alexander bodies featured a shallow, full-width destination box. Later a deeper box was made available, although the glass of this box was a little narrower, within the full-width panelling, leaving room for marker lights on either side. The top of this box was slightly higher than the roof-line but was faired into the roof neatly. An optional rear display stood proud of the roof. Although square-cornered side glazing was still available initially, production bodies now most commonly had round-cornered side windows.

Above: This bus has the very first Alexander body to be mounted on a Mercedes-Benz T2 chassis-cowl. Burnley & Pendle Transport 91 (E91 LBV) was the first of four examples, new in February 1988. The windscreen is the standard unit supplied with the chassis-cowl. *The late Derek Took.*

Below: This long wheelbase 811D, Ulsterbus 44 (MJI 3341), came into the fleet with the business of Donnell of Strabane. Like the prototype body on 709D E40 OMS, this bus has the optional square-cornered side windows. A deeper destination box was soon to be offered.

NOT IN NOTTINGHAM

Burnley & Pendle's ground-breaking Alexander-bodied 709Ds were in practice preceded from November 1987 by six T2s with another make of body. These were numbered 84 (E84 HRN), a 709D, and 85-90 (E85-89 HRN and E90 JHG), which were 811Ds of the original short wheelbase model. All had bodywork built by **Robin Hood**. The name Robin Hood is most frequently associated with a mischievous character who, allegedly, got up to all sorts of antics in a forest in Nottinghamshire several hundred years ago. There are, though, real members of the Hood family who have been given the forename Robin. The Robin Hood with whom we are concerned had a grounding of coachbuilding by working for Strachans at Hamble, in Hampshire. Strachans had been supplying a varied range of bodies for many years, to operators including London Transport. Robin Hood had left Strachans in 1970, then set up Robin Hood Vehicle Builders in nearby Fareham in 1973. In August 1984, new premises were opened at Locks Heath, near Portsmouth.

Before long, Robin Hood Vehicle Builders was among several firms that turned to converting Ford Transit parcel vans and Mercedes-Benz L608Ds into minibuses, to cater for the 'boom'. The company's first involvement with Mercedes-Benz T2 PSVs was in the conversion of 609D van shells to 20-seat buses, for delivery in September and October 1987 to the Thames Valley & Aldershot Omnibus Company (trading

Already in the Burnley & Pendle fleet when the Alexander-709Ds arrived were six Mercs with bodywork by Robin Hood Vehicle Builders. No.89 (E89 HRN) was one of five on short wheelbase 811D chassis. Robin Hood, however, inaugurated the idea of a 'long tailed' body on this wheelbase, to offer 29 seats. Note the distinctive location for the destination screen. The different contours of the bodywork on this fleet's Mercs presented problems to the painters. *John Young.*

as Alder Valley) and South Wales Transport. By now, Robin Hood was making coach-built bodywork for the smaller Iveco 49-10 chassis-cowls (i.e., 4.9 tonne, 100bhp). These bodies, which were named 'City Nipper', were probably the most attractive on this chassis and, although rather flat-sided, the large principal side windows usually had rounded corners and aesthetically there was just the right depth of panelling between these windows and the edge of the roof. A novel feature was that the (shallow) destination equipment was affixed *inside* the top of the tall windscreen, allowing the glazing to reach the leading edge of the roof.

It was this body that was adapted and enlarged to suit the Mercedes-Benz T2. The destination box was again installed inside the top of a suitably heightened windscreen, which had a notably arched top, yet was set between the standard windscreen corner pillars that came with the chassis-cowl. This windscreen and destination-box arrangement made the Robin Hood body instantly identifiable.

A most interesting aspect of the Burnley & Pendle buses was that, despite the 4,250mm wheelbase of both their 709D and 811D chassis, they contained twenty-nine seats, rather than twenty-five. This came about because the bodies were longer at some 7,650mm instead of about 7,000, so they could accommodate an extra pair of seats on each side. The resultant significant increase in the rear overhang, by about 650mm, although legally permissible, could be problematical on the shorter wheelbase chassis when turning in tight places, due to the so-called 'tail-swipe', which could cause damage. Nevertheless, 'long tailed' 29-seat bodies were to become a very popular option henceforth, on 709Ds in particular.

Robin Hood seemed to be doing well because in 1988, a second plant was opened near Rotherham.

Robin Hood also offered side glazing with either round corners or square. This view of H422 GPM with South Gloucestershire Bus & Coach shows another option – that of a separate driver's door. As with the windscreen, the top of the rear window followed the well-arched roof-line.

FIRST EXHIBITION

The first public exhibition of fully-bodied Mercedes-Benz T2 chassis was the 1987 Coach & Bus Show, put on at the National Exhibition Centre near Birmingham that October. The Reeve-Burgess stand featured two Beaver-bodied Mercs, one on a 609D chassis-cowl and another on a 709D, plus a Beaver-bodied Iveco 49-10. Also exhibiting a midibus was Alexander, with their prototype body on a 709D chassis-cowl, which became E40 OMS, as mentioned above.

Another showcase event was the Brighton Coach Rally, held each Spring, and at the 1988 event there was a unique vehicle, entered by Bicknell of Godalming. E81 HPG, an 811D, had a coach body built by Plaxton, in which the shape of the windscreen was clearly derived from that in their Supreme VI full-sized (though long discontinued) coaches. Other features were adapted from the current Plaxton Paramount coaches.

CENTRAL WORKS DIVERSIFICATION

When the NBC's bus operating subsidiaries were being prepared for sale to the private sector, as part of the Act of Parliament that enabled bus services to be deregulated from October 1986, the so-called Central Works of several of the larger operators were set up as independent companies, even if initially retaining close ties with the operating side. Some of these works, now more correctly referred to as engineering companies, expanded their remit with the aim of surviving without the reliance on overhauling or repairing their associated companies' buses. The Central Works of Potteries Motor Traction (PMT) of Stoke-on-Trent became **PMT Engineering** and quickly saw a future in converting Ford Transit, Freight-Rover Sherpa, Mercedes L608D and even small Iveco 35-8 vans into minibuses. From here it was a natural step to head into the coach-built body market, not only on long wheelbase Freight-Rover Sherpas but on heavier-duty chassis-cowls.

The PMT 'Bursley' body, on 709D chassis, that was supplied for assessment by the Cheltenham & Gloucester Omnibus Company and resulted in an order for six more buses. Number 677 (F677 PDF) was allocated to the Stroud Valleys division. Note the forward-inclined destination screen.

The PMT 'Ami' body was essentially a coach, for the 811D chassis, so had eye-catching, sweeping looks. This example has the registration J7 FTG, chosen by its first owner, Flights of Birmingham, although it is seen here with Terry Jones's Vista Coachways of Yatton, Somerset.

In March 1988, PMT Engineering launched their 'Bursley' body, for the Mercedes T2 and for the Renault-Dodge 50-series. The name Bursley was that used by local author Arnold Bennett in his novels about the Potteries 'Five Towns', to disguise (poorly) the town of Burslem. The Bursley body was built on a box-section steel frame. The cant panels were flat but sloped gently away from the sides. The front of the roof incorporated a shallow destination screen, but a distinguishing feature was that this was inclined forward slightly, to give better legibility. There was a very large back window, with a slight 'peak' (overhang) to the end of the roof above it.

A 709D, seating 25, was completed as a demonstrator and was registered locally as E41 JRF. The next example appears to have been supplied in August 1988 for assessment by the Cheltenham & Gloucester Omnibus Company, which was considering moving away from their choice of the 25-seat MCW Metrorider. Numbered 677, it was registered by them as F677 PDF and it was joined by a demonstration Reeve-Burgess Beaver-bodied 709D, F311 DET, as number 678. When an order for six 709Ds was placed, it was PMT Engineering that won the body contract, for the Bursley body.

For their own fleet, PMT accepted a rather different-looking body from PMT Engineering, mounted on the 811D. This was called the 'Ami' and the treatment of the front end was possibly influenced by the Optare StarRider, in having an elongated sloping nose, in place of the usual cowl. The windscreen, though, continued up to the leading edge of the roof, with the destination display within the screen. Thirty-six PMT Ami bodies were soon produced for the PMT fleet, but it was also offered generally. Despite a strong start, PMT bodywork turned out to be a rare choice.

AND ANOTHER CENTRAL WORKS

The first Central Works to be set aside from its operating companion was also located in the Midlands. This was a much larger concern, having catered for the huge Midland Red company (the Birmingham & Midland Motor Omnibus Company) and the site was known as Carlyle Road Works. Midland Red was the first NBC company to be split up into smaller units, this being done in 1981, well before any idea of privatisation was ever dreamt of; it was done to improve the viability of the operations, the smaller businesses proving to be more cost-effective. The engineering side became, simply, **Carlyle Works, Ltd**. Again, the business turned to converting vans to early minibuses, although a body was developed for mounting on Freight-Rover Sherpa or Iveco 49-10 chassis-cowls. In March 1987, Carlyle Works was sold by the NBC to Frontsource Ltd, which was in business to acquire such engineering works.

In late 1988, Carlyle built their first separate body for a Mercedes-Benz chassis-cowl. It used a welded frame, constructed from Cromweld stainless-steel, which incorporated chromium for corrosion resistance. This was supplied by Cromweld Steels Ltd of Stoke-on-Trent. External panelling was, as usual, in aluminium, while GRP was used for various mouldings. The Carlyle product was very distinctive, but rather severe. The body sides were flat, yet gradually tapering, above which there were flat, angled, cove panels. A very boxy mounting for the destination-blind equipment stood proud at the front and the side windows were square-cornered.

Carlyle's van-conversions had been given type reference numbers in a series starting at C1 and these were carried as part of the body-numbers. The first of the new bodies, mounted on a short wheelbase 811D, was a C19, having the body-number C19.000 – the series was possibly unique in not starting at 001. Containing 24 coach seats,

Carlyle bodywork had quite severe styling, with lots of straight lines and sharp angles. The solid panel between the driver's window/door and the main side windows identifies this example as a C19, on the short wheelbase chassis. Thames Transit 402 (H103 HDV) is actually an 811D, however. It had been transferred up to Oxford from related fleet Red Admiral of Portsmouth. Much more emphasis has been put on Park & Ride provision since the 1990s.

this Merc was sold in March 1989 to Skill of Nottingham, by whom it was registered F79 KRA. Only one other Carlyle-bodied T2 was to receive an F-prefix registration, that bus being demonstrator F430 BOP, aimed at London operations.

A range of options had been drawn up. The C16 was for long wheelbase 811Ds, with up to 33 seats; the C17 was for similar buses, but with an extra-wide or 'double-width' doorway to meet London requirements (which will be dealt with shortly); the C19 was for the 709D or short wheelbase (swb) 811D, but in long tailed form, for up to 29-seats; and the C21 was for the latter pattern when equipped to full coach standards.

In August 1989, a C17-bodied 811D demonstrator, G222 EOA, was completed, after which general production started.

AN ULSTER BUS

In Ballymena in County Antrim, Northern Ireland, **Robert Wright & Son** had been building bodywork for mobile shops, mobile libraries and vans since the late 1940s. In the late 1980s, they turned to constructing bodywork for buses, albeit in a small way initially. In 1988, the local major operator, Ulsterbus, had enough faith in Wright to award them an order for 40 bodies on Mercedes-Benz 709D chassis; there was an understandable desire to secure employment for local work people. The buses, successors in this fleet to L608D van-conversions, entered service in 1989 as numbers 823-862, being registered in Belfast as NXI 6823-6862. Wright also impressed London Buses, winning an order for 16 wide-doorway 811Ds, which entered service in November/December 1989, as we shall see. A demonstrator to the London standard was completed in October 1990 and registered through the Ballymena VLO as IDZ 8561. These bodies were initially referred to as the TS-type, but soon received the name 'Nim-bus' (very often spelt as Nimbus and one of several uses of the name). In its body construction, Wright employed the well-respected and patented 'Alusuisse' bolted framework, constructed from interlocking alloy extrusions that were coated for protection against corrosion.

Busybus 862 (NXI 6862) was the last of the initial order for forty bodies to be built for Ulsterbus by Robert Wright of Ballymena. It was new in 1988. The styling was tidy and well-balanced. Destination display provision was subsequently improved.

The offside-rear aspect of the Wright 'Nim-bus', in 33-seat form, as mounted on 811D chassis. There was a simple, rectangular and fairly high-mounted rear window. L652 CJT was new to Southern National's Dorset area.

ANOTHER FROM EAST HAMPSHIRE
Wadham Stringer of Waterlooville, Hants, had a long history as distributors of cars and commercial vehicles, while they also developed a business of building ambulance bodies. In the 1980s, Wadham Stringer was building the Vanguard single-decker, but many bus bodies were of a welfare nature, capable of transporting wheelchair passengers who were helped aboard through a tail-lift. They also offered a midibus body, the 'Wessex', on Dodge, Freight-Rover and Iveco chassis-cowls. In 1987, Wadham Stringer made some Mercedes-Benz T2 vans into welfare buses for Avon County Council, then in February 1988 they announced that they were to adapt their Wessex body for the T2 chassis-cowl. Not surprisingly, a demonstrator was built, using a stainless-steel, box-section, riveted frame.

Registered in the November through Portsmouth VLO, F821 PBP was on a 709D chassis.

The first batch of Wessex-bodied T2s entered service in June 1989, as part of an order for twenty 31-seat 811Ds for Yellow Buses of Bournemouth, namely 40-49 (F40-49 XPR). The rest appeared in the August as 50-59 (G50-59 BEL). The bodies were rather slab-sided, but with large, round-cornered windows. Unusual sliding vents were fitted, as it was the quarter at each end that slid towards the middle. In a move that could be seen as denting the reputation of Wadham Stringer, Yellow Buses sold all twenty after only a few months' service. This, in fact, was the result of 'public dissatisfaction' with the principle of midibuses. Fortunately, Brighton & Hove willingly took them on (apart from 58, which went to Buffalo of Flitwick, Bedfordshire) and ran them successfully.

The Wadham-Stringer 'Wessex' featured large side windows and a deep quarter-light. Red Bus Services, of Clyst Honiton, Devon, bought J844 NOD new, in November 1991. The unusual window ventilators slid from either end, towards the middle. *Bristol Vintage Bus Group*

No more Wessex-bodied Mercs appeared until August 1990, when Plymouth CityBus obtained just two buses. The operator was keen to assess the T2 before choosing a replacement vehicle for their large fleet of Dodge 50-series/Reeve Burgess midibuses, although they were only four years old. Four Merc 709Ds were obtained, the first two having Wadham Stringer 29-seat long tailed bodywork (201/2: H361/2 BDV). The bodywork was little changed from the Yellow Buses examples but had conventional tipping vents and a larger destination box. The other two assessment 709Ds had Reeve Burgess Beaver 29-seat bodies (203/4: H683/4 BTA). The resultant order, starting with twenty 709D 29-seaters, yet with many more to follow, went to Reeve Burgess, for the Beaver.

A MOST FAMOUS NAME

Mention the name **Dormobile** and many would immediately picture a 1950s Bedford CA converted for use as a camper or sleeper van (hence 'dorm-mobile'). The company that made them, Martin Walter of Folkestone, later expanded into making personnel-carrier conversions as well. By the late-1960s, Dormobile had become the builder of the parcel-van bodywork on the then-new Ford Transit chassis-cowl and they further adapted many of those to minibuses for special, low-demand services. By the time the minibus boom started, Dormobile was well placed to mass-produce such minibuses. The next step was to produce a coach-built body for mounting on the Iveco 49-10 chassis-cowl. This was given the name 'Routemaker' but was disappointingly

DESIGN AND MARKET FORCES • 29

bland and square. Construction was in all-welded tubular steel, with GRP roof and corners. By now, Dormobile was owned by the Coate Group, but in April 1989, the business, said to be with record orders in hand (*Commercial Motor*), was sold to the Essex-based KBD Group. This was followed by the announcement that a new range of all-steel midibus bodies was to be launched.

Meanwhile, in 1989, a Merc T2 was given a Routemaker body, scaled up from that applied to the Ivecos, yet just as square. It was to be a demonstrator and was registered locally as F359 GKN. It was on an 811D chassis and was finished in light and dark grey, with a yellow zig-zag stripe and Dormobile names on the sides. It went to Milton Keynes City Bus, who bought it the following year; MKCB's fleet already contained T2s, as two years earlier, eight early Robin Hood-bodied 709D 25-seaters had arrived (66-73: E66-73 MVV; it is odd that so many early T2s had double-figure registration numbers). With MKCB, F359 GKN, which was numbered 74, carried at least three different liveries – white and yellow with Milton Keynes City Bus names, ivory and dark green Bucks Road Car colours and yellow and bright-blue MK Metro livery.

This bus turned out to be unique, because an all-new and greatly improved Dormobile 'Routemaker 2' was now announced. This was far more attractive, with gently curved sides and above the standard Mercedes-Benz windscreen this time, the destination box was contained within attractively rounded mouldings. Very deep quarter-lights were now featured. MKCB happened to be the first customer, in November 1989, with long tailed 29-seat 709Ds 93-97 (G93-97 ERP). These also turned out to be unique, however. By the time the second batch arrived, in May 1990 (98-100: G98-100 NBD), the side windows had been increased in height a little, so eliminating the deep cove panels and producing a very well-balanced design. (These actually followed a December 1989 demonstrator to this improved styling, G590 PKL.)

The first T2 to be bodied by Dormobile received an adapted 'Routemaker' body, as developed for the Iveco chassis-cowl. Registered by the bodybuilder as a demonstrator, F359 GKN soon passed to Milton Keynes City Bus, in whose MK Metro livery it is seen here. It remained a unique vehicle. *M.A. Penn*

Dormobile soon produced a new design, named the 'Routemaker 2', with much softer lines. It had very deep quarter-lights. After just a few had been produced, however, including Milton Keynes City Bus 97 (G97 ERP), the tops of the side windows were raised, to lessen the depth of the cove panels. This bus carries the Bucks Road Car livery. *M.A. Penn*

From this angle, the gentle curve of the body sides of the improved 'Routemaker 2' were emphasised by the discernible 'kink' in the glazing, level with the base of the tip-in ventilators. K982 KGY was new to Transcity of Sidcup, who were soon taken over by Kentish Bus, who then sold this 709D to Crosville Wales. The latter subsequently became Arriva Cymru – yet the eight-year-old bus is seen newly acquired by South Gloucestershire Bus & Coach, where again it did not settle, moving on to Faresaver of Chippenham, Wilts, this time for a longer innings.

As an alternative to the square-cornered side windows in the Routemaker 2, Dormobile offered round-cornered, rubber-mounted glazing. This is illustrated by L928 UGA with Phil Anslow of Garndiffaith, near Pontypool, to whom it was delivered new – a long way from its Glasgow-based supplier.

The Dormobile Routemaker 2 was offered with a choice of two styles of side glazing. The windows could either have pleasantly rounded corners, or they could be square-cornered, close-fitting and within their own metal frames. But due to the gentle curve of the body sides, the square-cornered windows took a detectable 'kink', level with the base of the tipper ventilator at the top of each window. Indeed, a dummy vent had to be installed in the narrow window of the emergency door and in the corresponding nearside tail window.

A most interesting event of 1990 was the decision by MKCB to have two of their L608D van conversions rebuilt with new Dormobile bodies. The original L608D cowl and windscreen were integrated into the somewhat wider new body which, otherwise, was of Routemaker 2 styling.

In August 1991, Dormobile changed hands again, when it was acquired by the FSV Group and retitled FSV Dormobile Ltd.

YET MORE POWER
Meanwhile, another option from Mercedes-Benz was that of a more-powerful engine. This was aimed for use in long wheelbase chassis that principally were to be completed as coaches, so containing heavier fittings. The same basic motor was now not only turbocharged but also intercooled – a system developed to counteract the unwanted increase in heat created when turbocharging the injection of fuel into the cylinders. Beneficially, the improved thermal efficiency produced more power. The output was thus increased from 115 to 136bhp at 2,600rpm, resulting in the chassis model code becoming 814D. This engine was designated OM364LA.

The *Baumuster* for the 814D was 670313. The first 814D coaches entered service in April 1989, with F-prefix registrations.

By now, fleet engineers were singing the praises of the Mercedes-Benz T2. They stated that it was very reliable, fuel-efficient and cost-effective. Drivers found it easy to drive and manoeuvre and a lively performer. Fitters found it easy to maintain. The only down side was that it was wider than the first-generation minibuses it generally replaced so, in a small number of cases, routes that had been opened up in tight places by minibuses had to be modified if worked by T2s. On the other hand, with their 25- to 33-seat capacity, these economical small buses took the place of larger buses on several light traffic routes and the model now became an integral and long lived part of many fleets.

ANOTHER NEW COACHWORK CONTENDER

C.G. Whittaker was a big industrial concern based in Sheffield, covering construction, haulage, car and commercial vehicle dealership and contract hire. A new division, **C.G. Whittaker (Coachworks) Ltd**, was incorporated in October 1983. Production, located in Doncaster, was also known as Europa Coaches. Geoff Whittaker recruited Alan White, the Transport Manager of Coachcraft (Doncaster) Ltd (which converted Renault Master vans for distribution through the dealers Crystals of Doncaster) to become Sales Manager.

The first involvement with Mercedes T2s concerned van conversions, but by 1988, Geoff Whittaker was concerned that his business was losing trade, because customers were turning, in increasing numbers, to Mercs with more-spacious coach-built bodies. He therefore advertised for a designer and the post of Engineering Manager was accordingly awarded to John Seale who had spent 23 years with MCW in Birmingham, where he had gained wide experience of bus design, more recently involving the integral Metrobus double-decker, in 2- and 3-axle form, and the Metrorider midibus.

While Seale was producing his first design for Whittaker's, an 811D chassis was bought, in preparation. This was lengthened to the 4,800mm wheelbase at Europa Coaches' factory, to Mercedes-Benz standards. Seale's design, though, dispensed with the Mercedes cowl, as the body featured a sloping front end, in the style of the Optare StarRider. Astonishingly, Geoff Whittaker even bought a StarRider for him to take apart, to see what could be improved upon. Seale's design incorporated a lifting bonnet, to enable routine checks to be made from outside the bus. The slope of the front required the air-cleaner to be relocated and this was done with Mercedes' approval.

The body was slightly wider than existing designs, but it was noticed that, as a result, the rear wheels tended to disappear from sight. Therefore, the skirt panels were tucked in and specially styled. An important fact was that the new body, in contrast to both the Reeve-Burgess Beaver and the Optare StarRider, deliberately had rounded cove panels. Although thought by some to be old fashioned, this shape came about as a result of analysis, back in MCW days, of why the square-edged Metrobus tended to pick up a lot of road grime during the winter. Seale's midibus design also incorporated rounded corners at the rear, both features also making the body less susceptible to the effect of side winds.

The finished product was named the 'Europa Challenger' and, only a year after he had left MCW, John Seale was very proud to see his new design on exhibition at the NEC, Birmingham, at the 1989 Coach & Bus Show. It was also testimony to those who constructed the body in Doncaster, as most had formerly been in a very different industry as coal-miners.

With an eye to the future, two experienced managers were recruited, both having formerly been with MCW and Reeve-Burgess. It was then calculated that to use the standard Mercedes-Benz front cowl would make construction less expensive. Because of the width of the body, however, new front wings would be needed, as a well as a wider windscreen than the one supplied by Mercedes. The outcome was that in early 1990 Whittaker launched the 'Europa Enterprise'. The Enterprise was therefore the only body other than the Reeve Burgess Beaver on the Merc chassis-cowl to employ a wider windscreen. Understandably, this screen was similar in outline to that on the Beaver, which could cause confusion at first sight, but the Whittaker body's destination box was narrower and more upright, while the glass had rounded ends. Meanwhile, the Challenger prototype had gone back into the workshops, where the sloping front end was removed, and the conventional Mercedes-Benz cowl was restored.

The Europa framework was of all-welded box-section steel, incorporating wax injection for corrosion protection. Exterior panelling was in aluminium, with GRP used for the usual susceptible areas.

One of the very first Enterprise bodies was on an 811D chassis, and it was completed with the aim of trying to break in to the London market. It therefore had a wide doorway and 28 seats. Registered in May 1990 through Sheffield VLO as G395 OWB, it went on demonstration to London as ME1. Another early Enterprise body was completed as a 29-seat coach, on 811D chassis, for Lancaster of St Mary-in-the-Marsh, Kent. It was registered in June 1990, also through Sheffield, as G659 OWF.

Registered in the autumn of 1990, amid van-conversions, were more coach-seated Enterprise bodies on 811D and 814D chassis, plus what are believed to have been the first bus-seated examples – 29-seaters on 709D chassis, H522/3 SWE. It was rewarding that the local Yorkshire Traction Company should take Europa Enterprise bodies on their 313/4 (H313/4 TWE), 811D 31-seat buses, as part of an evaluation exercise. In fact, it is believed that 314 was the bus that was built as the Europa Challenger prototype. Similar Enterprise 811Ds H641-4 UWE were new to another local stage-carriage operator, Globe of Barnsley, in April 1991. In the same month, a similar example was placed in service by Potteries Motor Traction (372: H372 MEH), despite their associated PMT Engineering having fulfilled most of PMT's bodywork requirements on Mercs.

A very early Whittaker 'Europa Enterprise' body was this example, on 811D chassis, G395 OWB. It was finished with a wide doorway as a demonstrator to London, before being sold to Great Yarmouth Borough Transport. It is seen here after the council sold the company to First Eastern Counties.

Above: Another early Europa Enterprise was H641 UWE, seen here later in life in Bath, with Faresaver of Chippenham. The Enterprise featured a wider windscreen than that supplied with the Mercedes-Benz chassis-cowl. This screen was similar to that on the Reeve Burgess/Plaxton Beaver, such as the bus behind.

Below: At the rear, the Europa Enterprise carried a large back window, with rounded top corners, which complimented the curved cove panels.

NEVER TOO LATE TO JOIN IN

Founded in the 1960s, **Mellor Coachcraft** of Rochdale was at one time owned by Henlys, the car-dealer giant. Henlys itself was part of the Hawley Group, as were two significant producers of coachbuilt hearses, Woodhall Nicholson and Coleman Milne, although the Hawley Group saw to the merging of Woodhall Nicholson into Coleman Milne, with the closure of the Huddersfield factory. Woodhall Nicholson had a brief interlude in the PSV world in the late 1940s, becoming well known for thoroughly reconstructing the bodywork on several pre-war single-deckers for United Automobile Services of Darlington, some of the bodies later being transferred to *new* Bristol L5G chassis. In June 1989, the Hawley Group sold Henlys, Coleman Milne and Mellor to the major coachbuilders Plaxton of Scarborough. Mellor at this time was only doing van-conversions, primarily to welfare standards, so there was no clash with the Plaxton PSV range, which, of course, included the Reeve Burgess Beaver midibus. In October 1989, an extension to the Mellor plant in Rochdale was opened. In 1992, Plaxton sold Mellor and Coleman Milne to a resurrected Woodhall Nicholson, which was now a holding company registered at Westhoughton in Bolton; Woodhall Nicholson still owns Mellor to this day.

Mellor, meanwhile, had become one of the many to convert Ford Transit parcel-vans to minibuses in the mid-1980s. A major customer was Devon General, who then went on to contract Mellor to build the bodies on all their uncommon Mark III or VE6 Transit minibuses. Mellor also produced a large number of minibuses for

Built originally as a Council welfare bus, with a wheel-chair lift and door in the centre of the rear wall, G900 TJA is believed to have been the first coach-built body on Mercedes chassis to have been constructed by Mellor. It was later converted to a 32-seat PSV, operating for some time in the north Midlands before acquisition by South Gloucestershire Bus & Coach, where it carried a unique livery.

36 • THE MERCEDES-BENZ MIDIBUS

welfare organisations, some being conversions of Mercedes T2 vans. In 1990, however, something rather larger was produced, being a full-sized body on a Merc 811D chassis-cowl. It was registered by Mellor through Manchester VLO as G900 TJA and was supplied as a welfare bus to Gloucestershire County Council, with 16 seats and a tail-lift for wheelchairs.

It was not until September 1993 that the first examples of a revised style of Mellor body were built on Mercedes-Benz T2 chassis-cowls. Even then, these were to welfare standards and the upper fixing rail for wheelchair attachment resulted in the bodies having quite a high waistline. The front of the roof had no provision for a destination box. Their two major customers were Avon County Council and the London Borough of Islington, the first deliveries having L-prefix registrations.

Exactly a year later, the first examples to full PSV standards entered service. As it happened, they were for bus routes that Avon County Council financially supported. The buses were owned by Eurotaxis of Harry Stoke, near Bristol, which traded as Swift Link. Dealer-registered as M45-48 GRY (two-figure registrations again), they were 811Ds, comfortably fitted out with 33 coach-type seats. With no need for wheelchair fixing rails, the waistline was lower than in the welfare form, which enhanced the looks. The full-sized destination box at the front, with an upright face, was attractively faired into the roof, while the bodies also featured not only a rear destination box, but one at the side, as well. There was a Beaver-like ridge along the cove panels, to add style. The base of the quarter-lights was no lower than that of the side windows, though the driver's window did have a lowered baseline.

Mellor was so proud of these vehicles that one featured on their publicity leaflet. By the end of that year, eleven more bodies, on 811D or 709D chassis, had been built, all for customers in west Wales – Jones of Newchurch, Davies of Pencader and Silcox of Pembroke Dock. Two long tailed

Mellor later launched an all-new body for the Merc, as shown by N627 BWG, an 811D 31-seater. It is shown here after acquisition by Eurotaxis of Harry Stoke, Bristol – already a good customer for Mellor. The bus is in Blagdon, Somerset, on a Council-supported route. Note the unusual deep window alongside the driver's seat.

DESIGN AND MARKET FORCES • 37

709Ds were built for stock, but were quickly sold to Eurotaxis, again.

Mellor employed welded framework, using Cromweld corrosion-resistant chromium-steel. Side panelling was in aluminium, which was bonded to the framework, so that it was free of protruding fastener heads.

A BUILDER OF CARRIAGES.

Leicester Carriage Builders had dabbled in van-to-minibus conversions in the early 1990s, for the welfare sector. It then developed a coach-built body for the Mercedes T2, with a tail-lift for wheelchairs. In 1994, however, Leicester Carriage Builders won an impressive order for twenty 23-seat PSV bodies, on Mercedes-Benz 709D chassis, from Dublin Bus (*Bus Atha Cliath*), in Éire. These entered service from May 1994, numbered ML1-20. There was a follow-up order the next year, for fifteen 31-seaters on 811D chassis, ML21-35.

Ten similar buses arrived later for *Bus Éireann*, to work in Cork and Limerick, which took the total up to 45 bodies. Fuller details of the Mercedes midibuses in Éire appear below, under the heading 'Irish Interlude'.

The Leicester Carriage Builders body was characterised by having flat sides, although tapered inwards from half-way up the side-panels. The corners of the side windows had a large radius curve. The front wings were very distinctive, with a tapering grooved pattern at the top.

The only significant order for PSVs from an operator in Britain came from Leicester's local subsidiary of the then British Bus group, Midland Fox. This order showed support for local industry, yet it called for just six buses. These were 25-seat 709Ds, numbered M323-M328 (L323-8 AUT) and they entered service in July 1994. A later example, however, which was built as a demonstrator for Mercedes-Benz, yet registered by L.C.B., again through Leicester, as N331 OFP, also ran

Leicester Carriage Builders enjoyed much more success with Merc PSVs in the Republic of Ireland than they did at home. Of the forty-five bodies supplied there, ten were delivered to *Bus Éireann* on 811D chassis, including ML110 (97-L-1090). Note the well-rounded corners to the side windows. The strap line on the side interprets as Service (for the) Town of Navan. *Paul Savage*

for Midland Fox in their yellow and red livery. Midland Fox later became an Arriva subsidiary.

The only other contiguous batch of PSVs comprised N854-7 PDW for Shamrock (Jones) of Pontypridd, licensed in early 1996.

Leicester Carriage Builders' main business was in the welfare sector, and they continued to construct such bodies in some numbers.

WHO WAS MISSING?

We have now considered twelve bodybuilders that had turned to constructing coachwork for Mercedes-Benz chassis-cowls. Interestingly, of those twelve, only Alexander was a long established and high-profile builder of conventional full-sized single- and double-deck bodies, in which business it is still thriving as this is written, now under the banner of Alexander-Dennis Ltd (ADL). For some reason, none of the other established bus bodybuilders that were still in business in the late-1980s and early-1990s got involved with the Mercedes-Benz. This was especially intriguing when considering that both East Lancashire Coach Builders of Blackburn and the Northern Counties Motor & Engineering Company of Wigan had been involved with building midibus bodies for the Dodge/Renault 50-series chassis, the S75 version of which was close to the Merc 709D in terms of gross vehicle weight and dimension.

MERCS FOR LONDON BUSES

The powers that prevailed over bus operation in London evidently did not see the minibus boom as applicable to the metropolis, although small numbers were used for specific schemes in the suburbs, mainly on demand-responsive routes. Later, more extensive midibus schemes were introduced, utilising principally the Iveco 49-10/Robin Hood, Optare CityPacer, or MCW Metrorider. In July 1988, though, four examples of the Mercedes-Benz 811D-based Optare StarRider were chosen for a service in Catford. They had only 26 seats while, especially for London, the

London Buses chose the distinctive-looking Optare StarRider for their first wave of midibus conversions. SR104 (G104 KUB) is seen at Edgware Station. It was London practice in their midibuses to specify a wide doorway and only 26 or 28 seats. *Nigel Eadon-Clarke*

entrance was somewhat wider than normal, described as being of 'double width'. The buses were numbered SR1-4 (E711-4 LYU). The model evidently impressed London Buses and before long the class had multiplied and reached number SR123. The balance had F- and G-registrations, most of which were obtained by Optare, through Leeds VLO. These buses were employed on schemes in the West End, Peckham, Walthamstow and Harrow and also in the Bexleybus scheme, for which SR54-59 carried a blue and cream livery.

This size of bus, with wide-doorway 26/28-seat bodywork, certified for another 15 to stand, yet leaving circulating space around the doorway, was then chosen for the controversial replacement of Routemaster double-deckers on two busy routes in west-central London, albeit on a significantly higher frequency. These were the 28 (Wandsworth-Kensington-Golder's Green) and 31 (Chelsea-Kensington-Camden Town), with further examples required for an Uxbridge scheme. The choice fell to the 811D again, but this time with Alexander bodywork. Placed in service in late 1988/early 1989, they were numbered MA1-MA107, their registrations, obtained by Alexander, being F601-707 XMS. However, there was a glitch that was only cleared up by some renumbering – MA46-55 ended up being registered F946-955 BMS. Eventually the class total beat that of the Optare StarRiders, by reaching MA134 (MA108-134 were registered locally, as G108-124 PGT and H425-434 XGK). The F-registered buses featured square-cornered side windows, but MA108-134 had the more familiar and pleasant-looking rounded corners.

In July 1989, a demonstrator was received from Carlyle, also with a wide-door 28-seat body on 811D chassis. Registered by Carlyle through

A second supplier chosen for a sizeable fleet of wide-door Merc 811Ds for London Buses was Alexander. MA31 (F631 XMS), with Gold Arrow branding, is seen in Kensington High Street on route 28, on which these midibuses replaced Routemaster double-deckers. Note the square-cornered side windows and a slightly deeper destination box than used initially. *John Young.*

A second batch of Alexander-811Ds had the more-familiar rounded window corners, as shown here. MA109 (G109 PGT) is seen in Mitcham in its second month of service. *Nigel Eadon-Clarke.*

Birmingham as F430 BOP, London Buses gave it the appropriate number of MC1. Beside the coach supplied to Skills of Nottingham and mentioned before, this was the only F-registered Carlyle-bodied Mercedes-Benz bus. MC1 did not keep this registration, though, because after being bought in April 1990, it was graced with an old Routemaster registration, WLT 491. In time, that mark was transferred to another bus and the Merc received the new, local registration of F286 KGK. Meanwhile, in August 1990, London Buses followed up MC1 with four more examples, as MC2-5 (H882-5 LOX). No more examples were to be ordered from Carlyle, however.

In November 1989, five 709Ds with Reeve Burgess Beaver bodies were placed in service on a special Southall Shuttle service, for which the bodies had tail lifts for wheelchairs and only 20 seats. They were numbered MT1-5 (F391-5 DHL, issued through Sheffield). MT6 (F396 DHL) was an 811D, though, with 33 coach seats, for special use. MT7 and 8 (G537/8 GBD) were obtained to augment MT1-5. Another one-off 811D/Beaver, though a 29-seat bus, was numbered MTL1 (G621 XLO). It was later followed by MTL2-5 (G222 KWE, H189/91/2 RWF), while the initial 811D, MT6, was then reclassified as MTL6.

In Catford, another new set of routes needing wide-door 26-seat 811Ds started in December 1989. This time, the order was placed with Wright, so the buses were numbered MW1-16. As was

DESIGN AND MARKET FORCES • 41

Understandably, other coachbuilders were keen to gain orders from London Buses, so sent demonstrators which were built to full London specification. Carlyle sent F430 BOP, which became MC1, but they were not to be graced with a large order – only four more examples were delivered. *Author's Collection*

customary for Wright products initially, they were registered at Ballymena, as HDZ 2601-16.

Demonstrators continued to be assessed. In April 1990, an 811D with Whittaker's Europa Enterprise 28-seat body was received, so it was numbered ME1 (G395 OWB). This was not taken into stock, however, and was later sold to Great Yarmouth Borough Transport. It was followed in the October by Wright's demonstrator IDZ 8561. This received the temporary number MW00 while in London. Another one-off, MW17 (LDZ 9017, which will be described more fully later), came in 1992, then another order was placed with Wright for twenty more 811Ds. These became MW18-37 in 1993 (NDZ 7918-37, except that MW29 was NDZ 2629). The bodies on these buses differed slightly, in that to the rear of the wide doorway there was now a full-sized window, to accommodate the side destination box, so the half-bay was repositioned to its right. The offside of the body, however, was not altered.

Wright, on the other hand, did have more luck, as their initial order for sixteeen was followed by a further twenty-one buses. One of the 1993 order, MW22 (NDZ 7922) at Potters Bar, shows that for this batch Wright re-aligned the near-side body pillars to provide a full-sized window, with its destination screen next to the door, the half-bay now appearing beyond that. *Nigel Eadon-Clarke*

ANOTHER NEW CHASSIS VARIATION

In 1991, Mercedes-Benz announced that they were to make available, in any given weight range, the next most powerful engine up from the current maximum unit for that weight, as a standard option. In this way, the turbocharged 115bhp OM364A was to be made available in the 7-tonne chassis. The result was, of course, the 711D. The *Baumuster* for the 711D was entirely predictable – 669303. As with the 814D, the new 711D was particularly aimed at coaching applications, with up to 25 or 29 seats, depending on body length.

SPOILT FOR CHOICE?

So now, taking into account chassis and body availability, there was an enormous range of Mercedes-Benz T2s for operators to choose from.

Five chassis-cowls were available to receive coach-built midibus bodies, the models being the 609D, 709D, 711D, 811D and 814D. There were two wheelbase options and three choices of bodywork length. Added to that were no fewer than a dozen producers of coach-built bodies – this was the highest number of separate coachbuilders that the UK had witnessed for very many years, and it had to be good for British industry.

But was it too much?

AN UNSETTLED INDUSTRY

Building bespoke bodywork for the Mercedes-Benz T2 gave welcome choice to many operators, large and small. On the other hand, the fact that twelve firms were in the coachbuilding business, competing against each other for what was, in fact, a fairly small market, must have been seen as unsustainable by industry watchdogs. Some manufacturers, by offering PSVs among welfare buses, ambulances, van bodies and other coachwork, may have had enough custom to keep them busy but, with such diversification and varied stocks of specialist items being kept, profit margins could only be low. It should not have been a surprise, therefore, when bodybuilders got into difficulty.

The first casualty was Robin Hood Vehicle Builders, despite the optimism shown by the opening of their second manufacturing base near Rotherham in 1988. As early as 1989, Robin Hood ceased trading. However, with willing management and careful financial calculating, the Rotherham plant was soon up and running again, but under a new and rather grand name of **Phoenix International Coachbuilders**. Interestingly, the registered address was in Southampton (and it later became Fareham). The bodywork by Phoenix on Mercedes T2 chassis was indistinguishable from the Robin Hood products.

Soon, Mr Robin Hood started up on his own again, with a competing firm named **LHE Vehicle Engineering**, based at Eastleigh, again in eastern Hampshire. The bodywork was almost identical to the Robin Hood/Phoenix design – but not quite. The first started to appear from the autumn of 1989, on both Iveco 49-10 and Mercedes-Benz T2 chassis-cowls. The biggest consignment went to Stevensons of Uttoxeter (who amassed an amazingly varied fleet of Mercs), totalling fourteen 29-seat 709Ds, 160-173 (G160-173 YRE), with a few others to follow. Incidentally, G160 YRE had the notable chassis-number of 669003-2P-000001. Numbers 160-3 differed in their frontal design and this will be discussed later. The only other known LHE-bodied Mercs went in August 1990 to the Bee Line Buzz Company of Manchester, becoming H129-136 CDB.

Phoenix itself only lasted two years and a receiver was called in in May 1991. A group of former Robin Hood employees negotiated to buy the jigs and moulds of the midibus body, to restart production by their firm, Pentagon Vehicle Builders of Southampton. The outcome was similar to the Robin Hood style, except for the use of a standard Mercedes-Benz windscreen, with a conventional destination box above it. Apart from M433-7 JPD of Tillingbourne of Cranleigh, few Pentagon bus bodies were produced.

The year 1991 also saw not one but two other names disappear. One was caused by the decision to close Reeve Burgess. This was not quite as drastic as implied, however (except, of course, to those who worked at Pilsley), as production was moved to the main **Plaxton** plant, at Scarborough. For a while, Reeve Burgess Beaver bodies had carried Plaxton-style body-builders' plates and numbers, sometimes in addition to Reeve Burgess plates and numbers. Helpfully, the Plaxton body-number format loosely described the body style, e.g., '92 7 MHV 0681' referred to a body built in the 1992 programme, 7metres long and with the M standing for Mercedes chassis. This therefore described an up-to-25-seat Beaver, alternative codes being 7.6 M (a 7.6m Mercedes, with up to 29 seats) and 8.5 M (up to 33 seats). Of the other letters, the final character V indicated a bus and Y a coach. The middle letter changed according to length or specification, but the explanation of other letters is too complicated to describe in this work. Production of the Beaver as a Plaxton product continued and in substantial numbers.

The third casualty was Europa Coaches, also in 1991. This was because the parent Whittaker business collapsed. The group included motor-vehicle dealerships and Mercedes-Benz acted quickly to recover their vehicles from these dealerships – cars, vans, lorries, bus chassis and even part-completed buses. The bodybuilding plant in Doncaster was promptly closed and all employees were put out of work. With a funding package obtained, however, Alan White and other managers set up a new plant not far away, at Hellaby near Rotherham. John Seale was then taken on as Design and Quality Manager. On 12 September 1991, **Autobus Classique** Ltd was founded. This firm was to carry on with the building of the distinctive Whittaker/Europa Enterprise style of body, in moderately updated form, while also carrying out van conversions.

With the demise of Whittaker's, some incomplete Europa body shells on T2 chassis that had been seized by Mercedes were sold through the liquidator to **Crystals**, the Doncaster-based van convertor that was mentioned under the Whittaker heading. Crystals was owned by Chris Springham, of the Dartford, Kent, minibus sales company. He had been buying van conversions from some of the businesses based in the Doncaster area and now decided he would set up a manufacturing base in that town himself, at Kirk Sandall, so attracting local skills to join his venture. Some former Whittaker men joined him and were tasked with completing these ex-Europa bodies, which they did. Everything about the design was copied – it must have been quite bizarre for John Seale to see buses and coaches that he had designed being built by a company in which he had no involvement. Another two rescued bodies were completed by PMT Engineering, in March 1992, for PMT's operating fleet (485/6; J485/6 PVT). The following month, a Crystals-bodied 811D was supplied to Silcox of Pembroke Dock (J387 ODE), with another following a year later (K651 TDE).

For John Seale, perhaps the best accolade came from Norman Cook, Yorkshire Traction's Chief Engineer, who said that when the Europa T2s came in for their mid-life overhaul, there was little work to do on them. They were solid, whereas the bodies from competitors on the same chassis required significant expenditure to rectify. That was vindication to Seale that he had done a worthwhile job.

Casualties in the industry continued, regrettably. In 1992, a sad decision was taken to close down Carlyle Works Ltd. Again, the

Following the collapse of the Whittaker business, forcing Europa Coaches to close, incomplete buses were sold by the liquidator to Crystals of Doncaster, for completion. A Crystals-bodied 811D is seen here, just after delivery to Silcox of Pembroke Dock (J387 ODE). Meanwhile, Europa Coaches senior management had formed Autobus Classique, to carry on producing the same distinctive design, but in another factory.

construction of the midibus body was rescued, but this time from a long way away – by **Marshall** SPV Ltd at Cambridge airport – Dormobile had also bid for the business. During the 1960s, Marshall had been heavily involved in producing a standardised single-decker bus for the British Electric Traction (BET) group of operators. After the BET was sold to the State in 1967, its subsidiaries became part of the new National Bus Company (NBC) in 1968. In the early 1970s, though, Marshall suffered from the NBC's decision to collaborate with Leyland over the building of an integral single-decker, the Leyland-National. Following this, the NBC removed the freedom that their operators had previously enjoyed, of placing orders with bus builders of their preferred choice. Marshall survived subsequently on bodywork for British military buses and export orders, with a short lived diversification into double-deckers.

The last few Carlyle bodies, long tailed 709Ds for Southern National and new in July 1992, with late J-prefix registrations, were completed by Marshall. Marshall continued with Carlyle's series of body codes – C16, etc. – and gained several fresh orders. Indeed, in 1995, a batch of Marshall-bodied Mercs was delivered for London service, to join the varied types recoded above. At the end of that year, the Centrewest division received MM1-6, again wide-door 28-seater 811Ds. Of course, these were very similar to Carlyle-bodied MC1-5 which are recorded above. Marshall obtained the registrations for MM1-6 – N521-6 REW – through their local VLO in Peterborough.

A SERIES 2 DESIGN

In February 1992, Wadham Stringer announced they were developing a 'successor to the six-year-old steel riveted design', which would become the 'Wessex II'. Framing was now welded in 3CR12 stainless steel, while the principal external panel each side was a single-piece stretched Zintec steel panel. The Wessex II had a very different look to the original Wessex. It was a rather square design and, in fact, resembled the Carlyle/Marshall body in many ways. Curiously,

The WS Wessex II differed greatly from the Wadham Stringer Wessex and had a curious resemblance to the Carlyle/Marshall product, only with smaller side windows. P490 TGA was one of several Wessex II-bodied Mercs supplied to operators in the Clydeside region, although here it is with Faresaver of Chippenham.

however, the windows were smaller and more numerous. A benefit of the new framework was that internal width was increased from 2,100mm to 2,220mm.

Wadham Stringer had been owned by the TKM Group for several years but in August 1993 the coachbuilding division was sold to the Universal Vehicle Group (UVG), who renamed the business as **WS Coachbuilders Ltd**, leaving the Wadham Stringer name for use in other activities. The Wessex II first appeared as a WS product when exhibited at 'Coach & Bus '93'. The Wessex II was then supplied to several small operators in the competitive Clydeside region.

The initials WS were replaced by **UVG** from late 1995, during N-registrations. UVG then decided to adopt new model names for the WS range, and the Wessex II became the UVG 'Citystar'.

CAPTURING COACHING CUSTOMERS

From the outset, a T2 with a separate body-on-chassis was just as suitable for coaching applications as it was for service bus work. Some body builders made a point of capturing the coach market by upgrading the bodywork markedly to cater for the more luxurious requirements. For example, the Reeve Burgess Beaver coach differed from the bus version in up to ten respects. The coach had a swivel-type single-piece door, instead of two-leaf folding doors; fixed windows, with opening roof-lights instead; tinted side glazing; coach seats, with high-quality trim to body side walls; full-length luggage racks; no ticket-issuing facility around the driver's position, so eliminating rails and screens; plus options of curtains to the side windows and in-vehicle entertainment.

From the outset, the Mercedes-Benz T2 with Reeve-Burgess Beaver bodywork was commonly chosen as a coach. Typically, this would be on a 609D chassis. But, despite the registration G609 THR, this is not a 609D, nor even a 709D – it is actually an 811D. You can't tell by looking. It was new to Levers of East Knoyle, Wiltshire, in 1990. By the time of this photograph, Levers had become a subsidiary of Wilts & Dorset, who never operated a T2 in their own fleet.

Above: On the longer wheelbase chassis, the Beaver coach could look very impressive. Geoff Willetts of Pillowell, in the Forest of Dean, Gloucestershire, ran this 814D, L353 MKU, from new in 1993. Although the Beaver service bus had gained a deeper destination box, coaches retained the shallow dome, although the screen was revised with rounded ends.

Below: Autobus Classique concentrated on the coach market. New in January 1993 was this 814D, with full depth glazing in the door, K838 FEE. As signwriting on the front wing states, it is a 33-seater. Note the 'destination box' is much neater than that on the bus version of this body design.

Autobus Classique, soon after its formation, concentrated on this sector of the market, for which the 711D was a widespread choice. As early as the spring of 1993, indeed, there came the Autobus Classique II, a coach in which the principal visual difference was that it had a shallow 'hi-line' back window. The Mark II was itself superseded in 1995 by the Autobus Classique Nouvelle. This, though, featured an enclosed, swept-back front end – albeit not a pretty one – to give it less of a bus- or van-like appearance. Incidentally, many Mercs with Autobus Classique coachwork were sold through dealers H & L Garages Ltd, who had outlets across Lincolnshire and Yorkshire. This resulted in many such vehicles being registered through Boston and Grimsby VLOs.

The Optare StarRider was available with a similar, luxury finish, to make it into a coach, and Mellor offered the same range of enhancements.

'FULL-FRONT' OPTIONS

The Autobus Classique Nouvelle followed the Optare StarRider and PMT Ami in dispensing with the Mercedes-Benz cowl entirely, by featuring an all-inclusive frontal profile. Other bodybuilders, however, adopted what might be called a 'full-front' style, by bringing the windscreen forward, to the front of the bonnet, just above the normal Mercedes radiator-grille. The first builder to do this was Robin Hood, who, in January 1988 supplied a short wheelbase 811D/29-seat coach with a 'full front' to Amport & District Coaches of Thruxton, Hants; the registration was reserved by Robin Hood through Portsmouth VLO as E533 JOT. Others soon followed, including short wheelbase 16-seaters E480/90/99 JLK, for Wings Luxury Travel of Hayes, Middlesex, and long wheelbase 33-seat coaches E198/9 LRV, two more with registrations reserved by Robin Hood, but for

To produce a coach, Mellor adapted their bodywork with the same range of upgrades as did other manufacturers. Note the last side window has a higher baseline, due to the last two rows of seats being raised, to provide a spacious boot beneath. Gwent Travel Services WJI 3725 was new as P973 YSB.

A very sleek-looking coach was produced by Robin Hood, by bringing a well-raked, curved windscreen forward, to the front of the bonnet. Access to the engine, for routine checks, was rather hampered by this layout, however. E198 LRV is a 33-seat 811D, new to W&H Motors of Horley, but here with Arnold Liddell of Bristol.

delivery to W&H Motors of Horley, Surrey, close to Gatwick Airport.

After Robin Hood Vehicle Builders failed, the 'full-front' idea was perpetuated by one of its successors, LHE Vehicle Engineering. This style of body was named the LHE 'Voyager' and appeared, as hinted at above, on the first four of the Stevenson's batch of fourteen, 160-3 (G160-3 YRE), albeit these were equipped with bus seats. The normal, kinked profile body was called the LHE 'Commuter'.

The other body offered in 'full-front' form was again just for local bus work, although on this body, the Wright TS or Nim-bus, the feature was known as the 'fast front'. From September 1991, fast-front versions of the 709D 25-seater were supplied to Ulsterbus, starting with 863-882 (TXI 7863-7882). Other examples were to follow.

One 1995 811D bus had additional interest by having the floor behind the rear axle dropped to a lower level, complete with its own doors at the side and rear. This was to allow wheelchair passengers aboard, because 1814 (HAZ 5814), was for use exclusively at the Giant's Causeway on the Antrim coast, on a special service on the steep hill between the visitor centre and the spectacular rock formations.

Wright built one fast-front 811D in 1992 to London Buses specification, with a wide-doorway and 26 seats. It entered service in the July and was numbered MW17 (LDZ 9017).

Above: Another builder to bring the windscreen forward was Wright, who used the standard Mercedes-Benz glazing for the 'Fast-front' version of their TS or Nim-bus body. This is Ulsterbus 886 (AAZ 8886), a 709D 25-seater, which is seen leaving Newtownards bus-station on a 'Town Service'.

Below: Fast-front 811D 1814 (HAZ 5814) had a specially lowered vestibule at the back, with its own doors, to take passengers in wheel-chairs down to look at the Giant's Causeway rock formations, on the Antrim coast. *Paul Savage*

AN IRISH INTERLUDE

Over the border in the Irish Republic, a business based in Donegal, in the north-west of the country, started converting vans into minibuses in the late 1980s. If that company's name, of *Euro Van Converters*, did not show aspirations, then the new name of **Euro Coach Builders** certainly indicated grander things.

It was a while before the company started constructing coach-built bodies, though. In 1993, Euro Coach Builders received a very gratifying order from the important Dublin Bus/*Bus Atha Cliath* organisation, for 20 coachbuilt bodies on Mercedes-Benz 709D chassis-cowls. They were for Dublin's 'City Imp' network and were to be numbered ME1-20.

Dublin Bus had started to run midibuses in 1990, by buying a batch of just ten Merc 811Ds. These were bodied by Wright in Northern Ireland, so were numbered MW1-10. They were registered in Dublin as 90-D-5001 to 5010. They converted route 83 (City to Kimmage) to midibus operation.

Following a three-year gap, in 1993 Dublin Bus received an MA-class of twenty Alexander Sprint 709Ds, also built in Northern Ireland (93-D-8001 to 8020). The first ten of the ME-class were then delivered, later in 1993, as ME1-10 and were registered 93-D-10001 to 10010. In 1994 there came ML1-20 (94-D-1001 to 1020), 709Ds with uncommon bodywork by Leicester Carriage Builders. These were intermingled with the ten outstanding 709Ds with Euro Coach Builders bodies, ME11-20 (94-D-2011 to 2020).

The styling of the Euro Coach Builders product bore a marked resemblance to the Plaxton Beaver, other than at the front end. The Beaver was noted for its wider-than-usual windscreen, of course, but the Euro Coach Builders product incorporated the standard Mercedes-Benz windscreen. Euro Coach Builders had ties with a distributor in Cork, at the opposite end of the country, yet this proved a successful partnership for supplying Mercs – mainly van-conversions – to numerous small operators throughout Ireland.

Bus Atha Cliath (Dublin Bus) started developing its 'City Imp' midibus network in 1993. Both 709D and 811D Mercedes were chosen, with a variety of bodies. This is ML9 (94-D-1009), a 709D bodied by Leicester Carriage Builders. It features their well-rounded window corners and their grooved moulding on the front wing. *Paul Savage*

Above: City Imp ME13 (94-D-2013) is another 709D, but this has Irish-built coachwork by Euro Coach Builders. Apart from the front end of the bodywork, there is a strong resemblance to the Reeve-Burgess/Plaxton Beaver. Note the *sliding* ventilators, rather than the usual tippers. *Paul Savage*

Below: The Euro Coach Builders body as lengthened for the 811D chassis. Bus Éireann's ME203 (97-G-1859) is seen at Dundalk, a long way from where it was registered – in Galway – four years earlier. *Paul Savage*

Pleased with the Euro bodies, Dublin Bus placed further orders: ME21-35 (94-D-37021 to 37030 and 95-D-31 to 35) were more 709Ds, while ME36-55 (95-D-33036 to 33055) were 811Ds this time. The quarter-lights ahead of the door/cab-window was deepened for these thirty-five bodies. Also arriving in 1995 were ML21-35 (95-D-5021 to 5035), with LCB bodies on 811D chassis.

Understandably, the national operator in the rest of the country, *Bus Éireann*, also took to the Mercedes-Benz midibus, but – surprisingly – not until 1997. In that year, *Bus Éireann* placed in service their ML101-110, Leicester Carriage Builders-bodied 811Ds. These were registered in Cork (97-C-4858/60/2-5) and Limerick (97-L-771/2, 844, 1090). Directly following these were more 811Ds, but with Euro Coach Builders bodies. ME201-210 were registered in Galway (97-G-1857-60/2/4/7/8) and Waterford (97-W-713/4). Another four of the latter, however, had been diverted at the end of 1996 to Dublin Bus, as their ME56-59 (96-D-50056 to 50059).

Euro Coach Builders supplied a further batch of Mercs to Dublin Bus after a short while and these will be discussed later in this work. The order, which was for a further twenty-five bodies, showed that Dublin Bus was very satisfied with the product of Euro Coach Builders The latter ultimately supplied more bodies than other three coachbuilders combined.

AN IMPROVED MERCEDES

In 1993, Mercedes-Benz undertook a series of revisions and improvements for incorporation into future production of the popular 7-tonne 25-to-29-seater bus. Significantly, the new variation was based on the 711D, with the turbocharged engine, but this was now made cleaner burning, to meet Euro2 emission standards. A demonstrator was prepared and Mercedes-Benz (UK) at Tankersley got it registered through Sheffield VLO as L707 LKY - how did they miss the chance to obtain the number 711?. Plaxton bodied the bus with a Beaver body, which was painted in Bristol's City Line livery, for long term evaluation among a fleet of 709D Beavers. It is interesting that by then, neighbouring Badgerline had already acquired a 711D as an evaluation bus (3877: L877 TFB).

The 711D was offered as an alternative to the 709D and before long, certainly by P-prefix registrations, the 711D was the rule, rather than the exception.

Incidentally, another demonstrator for M-B was L708 LKY, but this was an 811D with 33-seat Wright Nim-bus bodywork. As it happens, the demonstration duties of this dark-red bus also took it to Bristol City Line.

A MATTER OF CHOICE

Of course, any operator seeking a Mercedes midibus would choose the model best suited to their requirements. One NBC operator is worth mentioning because their requirement was for more power. This was South Wales Transport (SWT). The company had built up a large fleet of Mercedes-Benz L608D minibuses and was a natural host when the T2 came along. In 1987/8, after taking the four Robin Hood van-conversion 609Ds, mentioned above, there came no fewer than forty 709Ds with Reeve-Burgess Beaver B25F bodies. The company then decided more power was desirable. So, from number 323 (F323 DCY), the chassis specified was the 811D, but in its short wheelbase form and with the same Reeve-Burgess Beaver B25F bodywork. Similarly, when SWT turned to the longer Merc for 31 seats, from number 328 (F328 FCY), the chassis specified was the 814D and this version was chosen for all fifty-one 31-seaters.

The Transit Holdings group, with operations in Devon, Portsmouth and Oxford, was another to specify short wheelbase 811Ds, though these received long tailed, 29-seat bodies, by Carlyle.

The long tailed option appealed to Nottingham City Transport, but only as an afterthought. The result was that the 7-metre 25-seat Beaver bodies on their 709Ds were rebuilt to the 7.6-metre length, with long tails, to take 29 seats. The company had meanwhile turned to the long wheelbase 811D.

Above: Here is another example of 'don't go by its looks' – this 25-seat Beaver-bodied Merc could be a 609D or a 709D but, to meet the request from South Wales Transport for greater power, 326 (F326 DCY) is one of a batch of short wheelbase 811Ds.

Below: Similarly, SWT wanted more power for their longer 31-seaters, so specified the 814D. Bodywork by Phoenix is carried by 348 (G348 JTH).

Above: Nottingham City Transport considered their 25-seat Beaver-bodied 709Ds were too small, so lengthened the tail-end of their bodies, to make them into 29 seaters. And you *can* see the join.

Below: Probably the most peculiar Mercedes-Benz T2 to appear was this charabanc, CZ 1922, operated on Belfast sight-seeing tours. It actually started life as one of Ulsterbus' Wright TS-bodied 709Ds, 840 (NXI 6840) – see above – but after being nigh-on destroyed during the Troubles, it was rebuilt and re-registered as shown. It's just as well the Mercedes three-pointed-star was carried on the grille, as one would never have known. *Paul Savage*

MORE NAMES DISAPPEAR

It is particularly sad when a famous and long lasting business ceases trading, but this unthinkable event happened in 1994 to Dormobile. Having produced one of the best-looking midibus bodies for the Merc T2, the last few Dormobile examples entered service that summer, just attaining M-prefix registrations.

Even the ground-breaking Optare StarRider had reached the end of its production run, with the last bus-duty examples appearing as early as December 1991 and the last StarRider coaches in the summer of 1994 (just three gained M-prefix registrations). In 1996, however, Optare acquired Autobus Classique, whose Nouvelle fitted neatly into the hole left by the StarRider coach. The rather ungainly styling of the front end of the Nouvelle body may have concerned Optare, because the following year, they restyled the body entirely, to good effect, as the Nouvelle II. The reworking saw the product rounded, with a small, oval grille. It now had a distinct Optare look, much as had been the case after Optare had bought the MCW Metrorider design (which thus became the Optare MetroRider).

Right: Autobus Classique launched their new coach body, the Nouvelle, in 1995. It had rather unusual front-end styling. This 814D-based example, N780 LHY, was new to Eagle Coaches of Bristol in February 1996, with a spacious 29-seat capacity. Note the side lockers.

Below: Under Optare ownership, the Autobus Classique Nouvelle was completely restyled, as the Nouvelle II. W371 PHY was new to Coombs of Weston-super-Mare and is seen in Wells.

ALL CHANGE!

1996 was a landmark year, as Mercedes-Benz launched a new model to replace the ten-year-old T2. The new Merc was developed from the T2 and the van was little different in appearance, in fact. The launch came at a vehicle show in Hanover, but it was a while before a right-hand-drive UK midibus version of the chassis was ready.

The new Merc was given a model name, this time – the 'Vario'. This was in addition to the familiar type of model code. Adaptations introduced on the production line for the British and Irish PSV model resulted, for the first time, in the model-code received the prefix O, for a factory-produced Omnibus version.

The same two wheelbase options were made available – 4,250mm or 4,800mm – but all chassis were plated for a gross weight of just under 8-tonnes. The engine, designed to meet Euro2 standards of reduced exhaust emissions, and able to be upgraded as regulations became stricter, was a new product, the OM904, which was slightly larger than the OM364, at 4.2 litres. It had an entirely different sound, with a rather heavy tick-over, which caused no slight vibration. For the PSV version, this engine was usually turbocharged and intercooled (the OM904LA) and rated at 136bhp, which gave the new Vario bus or coach the code of O814D. More often than not, a badge was affixed to the grille and this simply stated 'O 814'. A lower power setting for the engine, at 102bhp (the OM904A), was available and the resultant code was O810D. However, uptake of the O810D was limited and, in any case, it is believed nearly all examples carried the grille badge of 'O 814'.

Discerning which of these two forms any particular Vario took was not helped by the *Baumuster* because, for the Vario, this took on a revised meaning and no longer could the engine power be ascertained from that. Instead, the meaning of the two Baumusters was:

6703<u>7</u>3 for the chassis with 4,250mm wheelbase; and 67037<u>4</u> for that with 4,800mm wheelbase.

A welcome new option was that of air suspension, which incorporated a kneeling facility, to ease boarding or alighting. Some T2s, particularly London 811Ds, had meanwhile been converted to air suspension. The Vario chassis frame design was basically unchanged from the T2, so it meant that, from road level, there were still three steps up into the saloon. Therefore, wheelchairs could not be accommodated in the standard body. At this time, disability awareness was growing and full-sized buses with a 'step-free' doorway and a flat, low floor were now being placed in service.

The T2's simple rectangular grille, with oblong headlight/direction indicator clusters either side, was replaced on the Vario by a deeper grille, with inclined sides and sympathetically re-styled headlamps and indicators. The bonnet and lower scuttle remained unchanged, though. The grille and headlight assembly of the Vario could, in fact, be supplied for fitting to T2s to modernise their looks, and, indeed, some T2s were adorned with Vario fronts, to give an up-to-date appearance, should anybody notice.

As before, manual and automatic gearboxes were available.

VARIO VARIETY

It is interesting to see how the Vario followed in the tyre-tracks of the T2 and to see what bodywork was available for the Vario, after so many coachbuilders had fallen by the wayside.

To go with the new model, three of the remaining bodybuilders refreshed their designs. These generally became more rounded in the process, to go with the styles of the day.

Plaxton extensively revised their design, with the aid of the well-known Ogle design studios, and named it the 'Beaver 2'. This body benefited from a slightly lowered window line, which allowed it to gain well-rounded cove panels now, these continuing through to the leading edge of the roof, so embracing the destination screen panel. The lowered window-line also enabled a rear destination and/or route-number box to be fitted, above the rear window. For the short wheelbase Vario, the Beaver 2 only came in 'long tailed' form. Strangely, this was 200mm longer than the long tailed Mark I Beaver, shown on the body-number plates as '7.8 M', i.e., 7.8metre Mercedes.

Above: The first examples of the new Mercedes-Benz Vario took to the road in early 1997. To go with the new model, three of the remaining coachbuilders revised their designs. Shown here is the new Plaxton Beaver 2, which, together with the long wheelbase O814D chassis, became the most popular option. R808 HWS, belonging to Andy James of Malmesbury, Wiltshire, is seen just over the Gloucestershire border, in Cirencester.

Below: The short wheelbase version of the Vario O814 is shown here by Blagdon Lioness Coaches S11 BLC. It is at Chew Lake, before setting off on the twice-weekly service to the seaside. Note the Beaver 2 transfers on the front wings.

This view compares the rear styling of the Beaver 2-Vario, on the left, with the original-style Beaver-709D on the right. They are Southern National 864 (S864 LRU) and Badgerline 7843 (M843 ATC), and they are seen in Wells, Somerset.

An important point should be noted concerning the Plaxton coach body on the Vario. Although the new Beaver 2 was supplied with the new Vario for bus work, for luxury coach applications of the Vario, Plaxton continued to produce the coach version of the *original* Beaver design, as had been built for the T2. Confusingly, several carried external transfers stating Beaver 2, which it was not.

The reason became clear in 1997, when Plaxton announced a new coach body for the Vario, named the 'Cheetah'. This design had a smooth, rounded, 'full-front' style of fascia, so as to be much more appealing to private-hire customers. In 2006, to provide a less-expensive coach, Plaxton decided to combine the front end of the Cheetah with the Beaver 2 body, and to call it the 'Beaver 3'.

Marshall introduced their 'Master', also with rounded cove panels (in stark contrast to its predecessor) and distinguished by a destination screen, within rounded mouldings, that was inclined forward; this presented a family resemblance with the Marshall Capital body on the new low-floor Dennis Dart SLF (described briefly later) and in fact, the backs of the two were very similar, having a shallower back window with a higher baseline. The framework of the Marshall Master was not significantly changed from that of the C16/C19 family. The Master had a different system of body numbering, though, starting at MST-001.

Alexander introduced their ALX100. As with the Sprint, the side windows (now square-cornered again) still reached up close to the roof but were deeper. There was a complete revision to the styling around the front of the body. The ALX100 was also wider than the Sprint.

Above: Initially, Plaxton's coach offering for the new Vario continued to use the original Beaver design. This is shown by R993 FOO, run by Chapmans of Tonyrefail, Mid-Glamorgan. The coach body, of course, retained the shallow destination screen, although it usually only carried the operator's name on the glass.

Right: Later in 1997, Plaxton launched a new coach body for the Vario, named the Cheetah. This was a much more aerodynamic and sleek body, designed to appeal to coach travellers. VX51 AWO was new to Marchants of Cheltenham in September 2001, so becoming one of the first to carry a registration in the new-style system.

Above: An un-registered demonstrator for the new Plaxton Beaver 3, being shown off in Weston-super-Mare. This design blended the Cheetah front-end on to a Beaver 2 body to produce a less expensive coach. This example was owned by dealers Mid-West of Cheltenham, who later registered it as VU06 KDX before sale, as one of six, to Hutchinson of Easingwold, North Yorkshire.

Below: Marshall's new body for the Vario, the Master, was much less severe than their Carlyle-based offering. The dominant forward-inclined destination screen may have looked a little uncomfortable, but it made the display commendably clear. The solid panel beyond the driver's window, on this short wheelbase chassis, shows the body framing was based on the C19. When photographed, S370 PGB was in the ownership of Eurotaxis, for Bristol city contracted services.

This pattern was only an interim design, however, because Alexander was busy preparing a family of ALX-coded bodies for the new, low-floor, fully accessible range of full-sized chassis, culminating in the ALX500 six-wheel double-decker, for Hong Kong in particular. After only 61 bodies of the original pattern had been produced, the ALX100 gained a new look, from the spring of 1998. The tops to the side windows were set lower down and plastic trim now surrounded these windows, similar to the other members of Alexander's ALX range. Even now, production was not sparkling, most being completed for the Arriva and Stagecoach groups. Those for independent operators took deliveries just into 2001 before production ceased, after a total of only 95 of this version had been built.

Robin Hood was back in business (briefly) and, in the late summer of 1997, launched the 'RH2000' luxury coach for the Mercedes Vario. It was a 'full-fronted' design, but without a Mercedes-Benz grille, due to having a curved 'nose', with a simple, slotted grille. The long, tinted, side windows now used curved glass. The coach was distributed solely by Stuart Johnson's 'SJ Carlton' dealership.

The designs of the bodies offered for the Vario by Mellor, the Whittaker design from Crystals, and the very small number of Leicester Carriage Builders bodies on the Vario, were unchanged from T2 production. However, UVG soon introduced a more rounded edition of their 'Citistar', but this was a rather heavy and clumsy-looking design. It was mainly supplied as a welfare bus. Construction was undertaken at UVG's plant in Bedwas, near Caerphilly.

Euro Coach Builders used their existing design for one more batch of Dublin 'City Imps', this time on the Vario chassis-cowl. They were numbered to follow the T2s, but with a modified

Bearing little resemblance to their Sprint body, the new Alexander ALX100 had flat, though inclined, sides and very large, square-cornered side windows. P113 HCH was new in June 1997 to Midland Fox but is seen while with Pete's Travel of West Bromwich and working in Bewdley in Worcestershire.

Above: A year after the launch of the Alexander ALX100, a second generation appeared. Its new, slightly shallower side windows had a plastic surround, similar to that on the new ALX200 to ALX500 designs for step-free, low-floor buses. One of several ALX100 Varios supplied to Arriva companies is Fox County (formerly Midland Fox) M151 (R151 UAL), seen in Leicester.

Below: This view compares the Alexander Sprint with the Alexander ALX100 from the rear. It looks likely that the rear window glass was the same on both, but nothing else was. Sprint N943 NAP was new as Stagecoach East Kent 943, while ALX100 R102 NTA was new as Stagecoach Devon 102. Both are seen here with ACL Travel of Weston-super-Mare.

In 1997, Robin Hood returned to building bodies on Mercedes-Benz chassis, with the RH2000 coach, for the Vario. An early example was R183 EOT, for Jones (Shamrock Coaches) of Pontypridd. Only a small Mercedes badge identifies the chassis-maker.

Mellor did not update their design when bodying the Vario. This is another to coach specification. The stylish slope now appearing beneath the shallower final side window (see above) is only the result of the application of glossy black paint. T979 OGA is on an excursion for Webberbus of Wheddon Cross, high up on Exmoor, to the historic city of Wells, also in Somerset.

DESIGN AND MARKET FORCES • 65

Above: Another unchanged design was the Leicester Carriage Builders body. In this long wheelbase version, the rear wheels have almost disappeared. New as S101 KNR with Kent County Council, it is seen here on Faresaver of Chippenham's private plate PSV 444, while at work in Bath.

Below: Also unchanged was the Whittaker pattern of body as built by Crystals. Here again, the subject is to coach standards. Gwent Travel Services' P3 OBS was new as P652 PFL with Smith of Coatbridge, east of Glasgow.

Above: Another Crystals body, and indeed supplied new to the Crystals bus-operating division in Dartford, is this 25-seater. Despite its looks, however, it is not a Vario. It is a 709D, new as N602 JGP, on to which a Vario front has been grafted, complete with an O814 badge.

Below: In 1997/98, Euro Coach Builders supplied another twenty-five bodies to Dublin Bus/*Bus Atha Cliath*, this time on Vario chassis. MV68 (98-D-1068) is seen here at an open-day. *Paul Savage*

prefix, as MV60-84. They were registered 97-D-50060 to 50064 and 98-D-1065 to 1084.

A REDUCED MARKET.

When it came to sales of Mercedes-Benz Vario midibuses, it turned out that the vast majority were completed with the Plaxton Beaver 2 body. The Alexander ALX100 was favoured by some Stagecoach fleets, of course, and even Arriva companies showed some support, but fewer than 100 of the revised ALX100 were built. A similar production total affected the Marshall Master.

The reason was that demand for front-engined midibuses was waning quickly. The Dennis Dart rear-engined lightweight single-decker was available in an assortment of lengths and could work many of the routes on which Mercs had been used (although there was a tendency to widen headways – the high-frequency of the minibuses was already forgotten). More importantly, though, from 1996 Dennis produced the Super Low Floor 'Dart SLF', with step-less doorway and a flat floor almost to the rear, making it fully accessible to users of wheelchairs (as well as parents with buggies) and thus compliant with the original terms of the Disability Discrimination Act. Other vehicle makers had similar buses on offer, although nothing approached the sales figures of the Dennis Dart.

Following that, Optare did what Optare do so well and launched the Solo, a midibus that, even with the front wheels right at the front, was fully accessible, with step-less doorway and a flat floor in the front half of the saloon. It had its engine at the back. Ironically, the engine usually specified was that of the Mercedes-Benz Vario.

For all these low-floor designs appearing, the straightforward nature and cost-effectiveness of the Vario ensured that sales remained steady, if not sparkling. After initial interest by the major bus groups, Varios went principally to small private operators who were providing rural bus work at minimum cost. As stated, most of these were completed with Plaxton Beaver 2 bodies and these were often furnished with coach seats, to give more comfort to passengers on such journeys. There were still several Varios supplied as coaches, not only with Plaxton Cheetah coachwork, but with bodies by some of the smaller builders, like Crystals and Mellor. These were similarly finished to a high standard of specification.

Mercedes-Benz later developed the Vario engine to suit tightened European emission levels, resulting in models coded O815 and O813, while Plaxton launched the striking-looking Cheetah 2 coach body. Later, some continental bodybuilders were contracted to supply rather more exotic Vario coaches.

But development of the Vario in the light of emissions and passenger access expectations meant that its future was surely limited. Indeed, production of front-engined Mercedes-Benz chassis aimed specifically at the PSV market ended when Mercedes-Benz ceased production of the Vario, the last entering service in 2014.

THE T2 OVERSEAS

It has been noticeable that despite a long membership of the European Union (EU), British ideas on the construction and operation of buses failed to impress Continental operators. There was no flooding of large towns or cities in mainland Europe with Ford Transits, Freight-Rover Sherpas or Iveco 49-10s. If there was a call for smaller buses, this was often met with midi-sized versions of big single-deckers, even to the extent of using the same large, thirsty engines. France, though, produced minibuses versions of Citroen, Peugeot and Renault medium vans and these vehicles, being front-wheel-drive, allowed a low floor and step-less entrance to be accommodated in their bodywork conversion. Seating may be as low as ten, but, in Continental fashion, there was plenty of standing space. These minibuses tended to appear on town services that never had more than a wide headway.

The Mercedes-Benz T2 chassis-cowl was, however, chosen when it fitted the bill, the vehicles frequently containing coach seating. In terms of engine performance, Continental

Above: At work on an infrequent town service in Les Sables-d'Olonne on the west coast of France, this Mercedes T2 has coachwork by the German builder Ernst Auwärter. The product is named the TeamStar in English. The design was also used for private-hire coaches and is very aerodynamic. This fairly early T2 was new 1987, being registered in France's Vendée Département, as 7002 SA 85.

Below: Setting off for a day trip with a small party of tourists, on the Mediterranean island of Menorca, is PM-6912-AY, a 1989 Mercedes-Benz 811D, with the short wheelbase. After 15 years of service, the two-doorway coach body by Spanish builder Ugarte is looking a little care-worn.

operators, in their full-sized luxury coaches, often choose higher power settings than in the equivalent British model and this also applied to their Merc T2s. A typical T2 would generally be based on the short wheelbase 811D, at least, if not the 814D.

Australia did show an interest in midibus operation, particularly in the suburbs of Sydney. Several operators chose the short wheelbase T2 chassis-cowl and these were bodied locally. These chassis, though, were sourced from the Brazilian plant of Mercedes-Benz and had different engines, so a different code was applied – LO812. The L-prefix had not been used for Düsseldorf T2 production, but the O was familiar, for factory-produced Omnibus chassis.

After the Stagecoach Group expanded into New Zealand and acquired the city operations in Auckland and Wellington, they acquired the operations in the Hutt Valley, not far from Wellington. Subsequently, several Stagecoach-standard Mercedes-Benz 709Ds with Alexander Sprint bodies were shipped across from their British subsidiaries to work for Stagecoach Cityline Hutt Valley.

After a full service life in the British Isles, a number of T2s was modified by dealers who specialised in used buses, such as Simon & Andrew Munden's Bristol Bus & Coach Sales, for export to African countries. Some dealers rebuilt T2s to left-hand-drive, with a right-hand doorway, for export to countries in eastern Europe.

Built for operation in the suburbs of Sydney, Australia, was this Brazilian-sourced Mercedes-Benz LO812. The bodywork was built by Custom Coaches, one of Australia's major coachbuilders. Note the rather upright windscreen. The example seen here, though, had finished work in Sydney and had been exported to New Zealand, for further service with Reporoa Valley Transport, near Rotorua on North Island.

Above: This stylish coach body, built on a Vario O815 chassis, was made by Portuguese builder Irmãos Mota & Ca Lda (Mota Brothers & Co Ltd), under their Atomic brand-name. Replacement small, round headlights have been situated lower down, although the original direction-indicators have been re-utilised. The coach was registered 82.44 QX in January 2001 and it is shown at work on the island of Madeira.

Below: The Isle of Capri demands small vehicles for its steep, twisty hills. Despite its looks, this, too, is a Mercedes-Benz Vario. It was registered in 2005, as CT-785LJ, and is coded O818 – 180bhp may no longer be a lot for a small engine, but, just a few years earlier, that figure was the output of the famous Gardner 6LXB that still powered many a British double-decker, from Bristol VRs and Daimler Fleetlines to Leyland Olympians and MCW Metrobuses. If you think the front-end does not seem like a Vario, look at those headlights and direction-indicators.

Above: More obviously a Vario, this O814 was built as an open-topped sightseeing bus, for operation in the narrow streets in the heart of the Czech capital, Prague. In the fashion of early British charabancs, it has a folding canvas roof for deployment if the weather turns bad.

Below: After serving their owners well, the time came to retire the Mercedes-Benz midibuses. Most were sold to dealers, who were experts in selling them on. In this view, in Bristol Bus & Coach Sales' yard, ten ex-FirstBus Mercs are neatly parked, hoping a buyer might come to inspect them. Many will go for scrapping, however, yet others may end up in a needy country overseas. All of these have Beaver bodies, except for one Alexander Sprint. Eight of them are 709Ds, while two are 811Ds.

SECTION 2
THE INS AND OUTS

PROMOTING THE PRODUCTS

All vehicle manufacturers produced illustrated leaflets or brochures to promote each one of their products. These publications also contained technical data and measurements, and a list of available options, to enable the potential customer to choose the most suitable model for his or her needs.

Mercedes-Benz (UK) Ltd produced wallets containing brochures that covered the entire T2 range. For example, the October 1991 wallet enclosed three brochures – one entitled 'for bus applications', one entitled 'for coach applications' and one described as being 'for vans for minibus conversion'. Each fold-out, six-page brochure gave an overview of the models in that sector, detailed descriptions of the engines and gearboxes applicable, comprehensive chassis descriptions and details of drivers' controls and ergonomics. There were also some photographs of completed examples of the relevant type of Mercedes-Benz.

Strangely enough, the buses illustrated on many of the brochures, from both Mercedes-Benz and the coachbuilders, had a leaning towards operators in the South West of England. The cover of the 1991 wallet is shown here. The main photo depicts Plymouth CityBus 709D/Reeve Burgess Beaver 207 (J207 KTT). The lower left picture shows twin Dartline of Exeter van-derived 609Ds, with locally finished 23-seat bodies by Devon Conversions. They are named *Denise* and *Anna* and were subsequently registered F950/1 HTT; note one has a folding door, while the other uses the original cab door. Lower right is a coach with Castleways of Winchcombe, Gloucestershire – an 814D/Reeve Burgess Beaver 33-seater, H383 HFH. Within the wallet, the cover of the 'Bus Applications' brochure carried the same photograph of the Plymouth bus, although for the June 1992 re-issue, its place was taken by another south-west bus, Badgerline's assessment 711D/Beaver 3877 (L877 TFB), posed against Bath's majestic Royal Crescent.

Separate technical leaflets for each chassis model were also included in the packs, with a cover photograph of a bare chassis-cowl. These leaflets not only contained technical descriptions of each model, but power and torque curves and dimensioned general arrangement chassis drawings.

Inasmuch as Mercedes-Benz produced brochures to promote its models, so too did the coachbuilders that had set up in business to body the Mercedes chassis. These leaflets tended to be double-sided single sheets but would carry a photograph of a typical body of their construction on a T2 chassis, with a table of dimensions, the construction characteristics, painting standards and optional equipment, plus line drawings of the bodywork. Occasionally, coachbuilders would reproduce a detailed report that was first printed in one of the trade magazines and which thoroughly described their bodywork. These reports usually included road-test results, as well.

Interestingly, Mercedes-Benz collaborated with some coachbuilders to produce combined brochures, promoting all models available with that make of bodywork.

Left: Seen here is the cover of one of the technical leaflets for specific chassis-cowls, in this case an 811D. As can be seen, Mercedes-Benz supplied their standard windscreen as part of the chassis-cowl assembly, and this was incorporated by most of the coachbuilders into their bodywork. Close study will reveal the chassis frame was slightly kinked over the rear axle.

Right: This depicts a brochure produced jointly by Mercedes-Benz and one of the coachbuilders, in this case Robert Wright and Son Ltd of Ballymena. Illustrated is London Transport's MW1 (HDZ 2601), posed in front of Stormont, the Northern Ireland Assembly's legislative building in Belfast. On the other side of this leaflet are bodywork specifications and dimensions, with some close-up photographs of specific items of interest.

Left: This leaflet was published by Marshall SPV Ltd, for the 29-seat 'long tailed' body for the 709D. The bus is another for an operator in the South West of England, Southern National. Although undated, the bus is doubtless one of their four J-registered examples, on which construction of the bodywork had been started by Carlyle. Bullet-points on the front emphasise notable features of the bodywork, while on the back, there are details of body construction, dimensions and basic chassis features, together with outline body drawings. The equivalent leaflet for the Marshall-811D illustrates what can only be North Devon Red Bus 750 (J610 PTA).

Right: Mellor produced a leaflet featuring one of their first production batch of PSV bodies on T2 chassis. The buses in question were 811D 33-seaters, for Eurotaxis (Swift Link) of Harry Stoke, near Bristol, later registered M45-48 GRY. Another leaflet was produced, illustrating a white, long tailed 709D, but carrying line drawings of both 709D and 811D models, with interior photographs showing both bus and coach-seated versions.

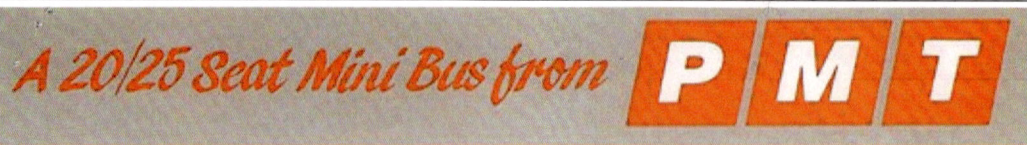

A 20/25 Seat Mini Bus from PMT

The Bursley Bus/Coach/Welfare Vehicle has been designed and developed by PMT Engineering and is built on the Mercedes Benz 609/709 chassis cowl.

ALL STEEL STRUCTURE
The all steel box section structure is jig built for maximum strength.

ACCOMMODATION
The wide body allows the provision of full size bus seating throughout.

SEATING
High impact resistant bus seat frames are fitted and allow a wide range of alternative material finishes. A full range of interior options from easy clean surfaces to full soft trim are available.

ACCESS
Wide 'easy rise' steps are provided at the front of the vehicle alongside the driver. Power operated doors are fitted to suit operators requirements. Jack knife manually operated doors are also available.

CHASSIS
The Mercedes chassis is fitted with a 4 cylinder naturally aspirated diesel engine developing 88 bhp at 2,800 rpm driving through a manual 5 speed gear box. All round semi-elliptic leaf springs with hydraulic telescopic shock absorbers provide excellent riding characteristics.

DRIVER COMFORT
The well laid out cockpit gives excellent all round visibility and a multi adjustable seat ensures maximum comfort.

WINDOWS
The large panoramic windows give superb all round visibility and are fitted in rubber gaskets for ease of replacement.

HEATING
Under seat heaters are supplied as standard (alternative independent systems are available).

VENTILATION
Lift up roof and/or Flettner rotary vents are fitted. Additional vents are available, as required.

SERVICING
Simplicity of basic vehicle design ensures ease of maintenance.

OPTIONS
A wide range of alternative seating, heating and glazing options for coach, bus and welfare applications are available. Automatic transmission and electric brake retarder can be supplied. Extended warranty also available.

SPECIFICATIONS
Seating: Up to 25 seated and 8 standees
Length: 6830mm
Width: 2286mm
Height: 2780mm
Weight: 3400kg (unladen)

For further information contact Barry Parkinson or Tony Marsh

PMT ENGINEERING

Woodhouse Street, Stoke-on-Trent ST4 1EQ
Telephone: (0782) 744744 Fax: (0782) 744244

This picture shows the reverse side of the leaflet for the PMT Bursley body. It can be seen to emphasise all the important aspects of the body's contraction, with some relevant photographs. Other coachbuilders' leaflets would address a similar range of features.

THE ASSEMBLY PROCESS

Photographs taken inside the factories where the midibus bodies were constructed are not common, yet are quite revealing. Taking shape here is an Optare StarRider. Although little work has been done to fit out the interior, most of the outside has been sprayed in primer. *Dr Mike Walker*

Some of the early Optare StarRiders for Badgerline are seen here, already painted into Badgerline's colours (one even with fleetnames), yet – as can be seen on the nearest bus – far from complete and not even glazed. This was the normal way coachbuilders proceeded with assembly. *Dr Mike Walker*

THE INS AND OUTS • 77

There was a tradition in the days when the Crossgates Carriage Works in Leeds was the home of the Charles H. Roe coachworks that completed buses would be posed for official photographs while standing by the front entrance to the offices. It was very apt that the same procedure was followed to photograph the first three Optare StarRiders to be completed there, for Badgerline. E800/4/3 MOU stand side-by-side. Initially, it was Optare practice to use the route-number tracks to display their body-numbers when first completed. However, there is a mistake here, in that E800 MOU should show 316 and E804 MOU should display 315. The error was corrected in time for some later photographs. *Dr Mike Walker*

Seen here in the Alexander (Belfast) factory at Mallusk is one of almost 900 basically identical, Sprint-bodied 709Ds that were built for the Stagecoach Group. As was the case at Optare, painting has been completed, yet not only have windows still to be installed, but the apertures for the quarter-lights and destination screen have yet to be cut out. *Paul Savage*

In Whittaker's Europa Coaches factory in Doncaster, the welded box-section steel frame for the flooring of a body is man-handled on to a Mercedes-Benz chassis. The body's upright pillars will be welded to the outer ends of this frame, before panelling for the floor and sides hides the frame from sight. *John Seale*

This doesn't look much like a bus! Seen here under construction is the prototype Whittaker coach-built body, to be called the Europa Challenger. The body pillars have been welded to the same type of flooring framework as seen in the previous photograph and now all are painted black. Well-braced front-end panelling shows the Challenger was to have a sloping nose, rather like the Optare StarRider and the PMT Ami. At this stage of construction, even the engine and radiator have been removed, to give free access to body components, for precise positioning in this all-new design. *John Seale*

It was a proud moment for John Seale when his design for a midibus body, now revealed as the Europa Challenger, appeared on a stand at the 1989 Coach & Bus Show, at Birmingham's National Exhibition Centre. It was painted in the midibus livery of Europa's major local operator, Yorkshire Traction. In the event, the Challenger never entered production and this body was rebuilt with a conventional front-end, as a Europa Enterprise. *John Seale*

This Europa Enterprise, while undergoing assembly, was whipped outside the factory for photographing. The picture shows clearly the principal features of the body's construction. *John Seale*

INSIDE STORY

The interior of a coachbuilt Mercedes-Benz T2 had the look of a full-sized conventional bus, only it was more compact. These midibus bodies generally had large windows, which made the interiors light and airy. Shown here is a Plaxton Beaver 23-seater, supplied on a 709D chassis to Badgerline, as 3905 (L905 VHT).

Bristol CityLine, for their Plaxton Beaver bodied 709Ds, requested a sizeable luggage pen, so limiting seating to only twenty-two. The pen, and an inward-facing single seat, are seen in this view inside 7872 (M872 ATC). This picture also shows the bulkhead that was fitted behind the driver's area, the full-height, glazed cab access-door, numerous hand-poles and partitions, plus the ticket-machine mounting platform. Seatbacks, body lining panels and the ceiling are all covered in a tough, woven cloth.

THE INS AND OUTS • 81

This is a coach version of the Plaxton Beaver, in 33-seat form, on 814D chassis. Besides the high-backed coach seats, the body features parcel shelves, tinted glazing, fixed windows with opening roof-lights instead, woven cloth coverings to the ceiling and parcel shelves, an entertainment sound-system and a complete lack of stanchions, or any bulkheads, screens and doors around the drivers' position. The coach is modelled by M766 WSC, which had been supplied new to Glen of Port Glasgow.

This is a Wright Nimbus 29-seat, 'long tailed' 709D. The rounded corners to the windows give a more relaxing impression than the square corners of the Beaver body. This example was supplied to Tim Jennings' Somerbus of Paulton, near Bath, as K29 OEU. It later became Badgerline 3916.

Here we see a Dormobile Routemaker 2 29-seater, with high-backed and well-padded seats, though without head restraints. The 'coach' impression is assisted by the lack of vertical stanchions, although rails along the ceiling would have assisted most passengers. In this picture, the gentle curve of th body side pillars can be detected. The subject is K721 HYA, owned by Coombs of Weston-super-Mare.

Turning to bodywork on the Vario chassis, this is an example of the most numerous variation, the Plaxton Beaver 2. It is a 31-seater, on long wheelbase chassis, new to the delightfully-named Flying Banana of Great Yarmouth, dealer-registered as P693 HND. Note the distinctive seat frames and moquette. The opening roof-light was an option. After Flying Banana was taken over by First Eastern Counties, this bus was transferred to First Glasgow, as MA243, though it was subsequently renumbered 50360.

Rather less common on the Vario chassis was the Alexander ALX100 body, in either form. This bus is to the revised design, as built for Stagecoach Devon, where it was numbered 102 (R102 NTA). Coarse grey fabric for seat backs and body lining panels was still very much in vogue. Orange labels at the front of the saloon, announcing fare deals, show the bus was now in the ownership of ACL Travel of Weston-super-Mare.

Another uncommon model of body built on the Vario chassis was the Marshall Master. Not only does it have a distinctive shape of back window, but the coves above the side windows are taken up with a bulky structure, more than necessary just for mounting the lighting units. The design is modelled by 27-seater S281 LGA, new via dealers Blythswood Motors of Glasgow to Cosgrove of Preston, later with Eurotaxis of Harry Stoke, near Bristol, but here with C.T. Coaches of Radstock, near Bath.

A fully-equipped coach body, including curtains and with no back window, is seen here in the form of a 33-seater Vario bodied by Crystals of Doncaster. The seat moquette fabric has been used to cover almost everything – certainly it is bright and cheerful. The coach was new as P652 PFL with Smith of Coatbridge, near Glasgow, but was working for Gwent Travel Services as P3 OBS by the time it was photographed.

CHASSIS AND BODY PLATES

This section illustrates some typical Mercedes-Benz T2 and Vario chassis plates, coupled with the relevant coachbuilder's body-number plate. They were photographed late in the vehicles' lives and, as the usual location for such plates was at the bottom of the emergency door, on the inside and at foot level, they tended to become rather scuffed.

The first specimen is from an early T2, new in December 1987. It gives the manufacturer's name as Daimler-Benz AG. The chassis-number, or VIN, has the country and maker identification letters W.D.B. – Germany, Daimler-Benz – already pre-printed on to the plate. The *Baumuster* and chassis-number appear without hyphens. The *Baumuster*, 668003, conforms to the model code, shown on the right, of 609D. The engine's power rating is shown in kilowatts, the preferred method used in Germany; 66kW is 88.5bhp. On the Reeve-Burgess body plate, note that the maker's name is outlined by the shape of a midibus – with six wheels. This Beaver 25-seat coach was registered E815 BMJ through Luton, for Jubilee Coaches of Stevenage.

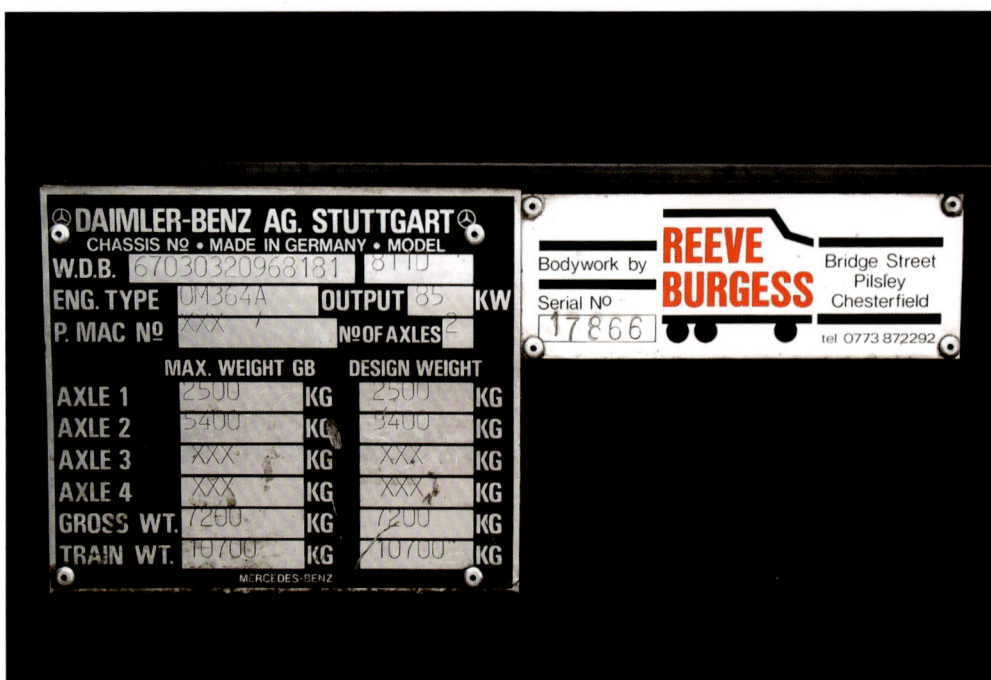

A few years newer, the plates on this Beaver coach show that it was an 811D, with the relevant *Baumuster* of 670303. The sturdier chassis is reflected by the greater axle ratings. The OM364A turbocharged engine is shown to produce 85kW, which is 114bhp. Also registered through Luton, the coach became H832 JNK with Anita of Sawbridgeworth.

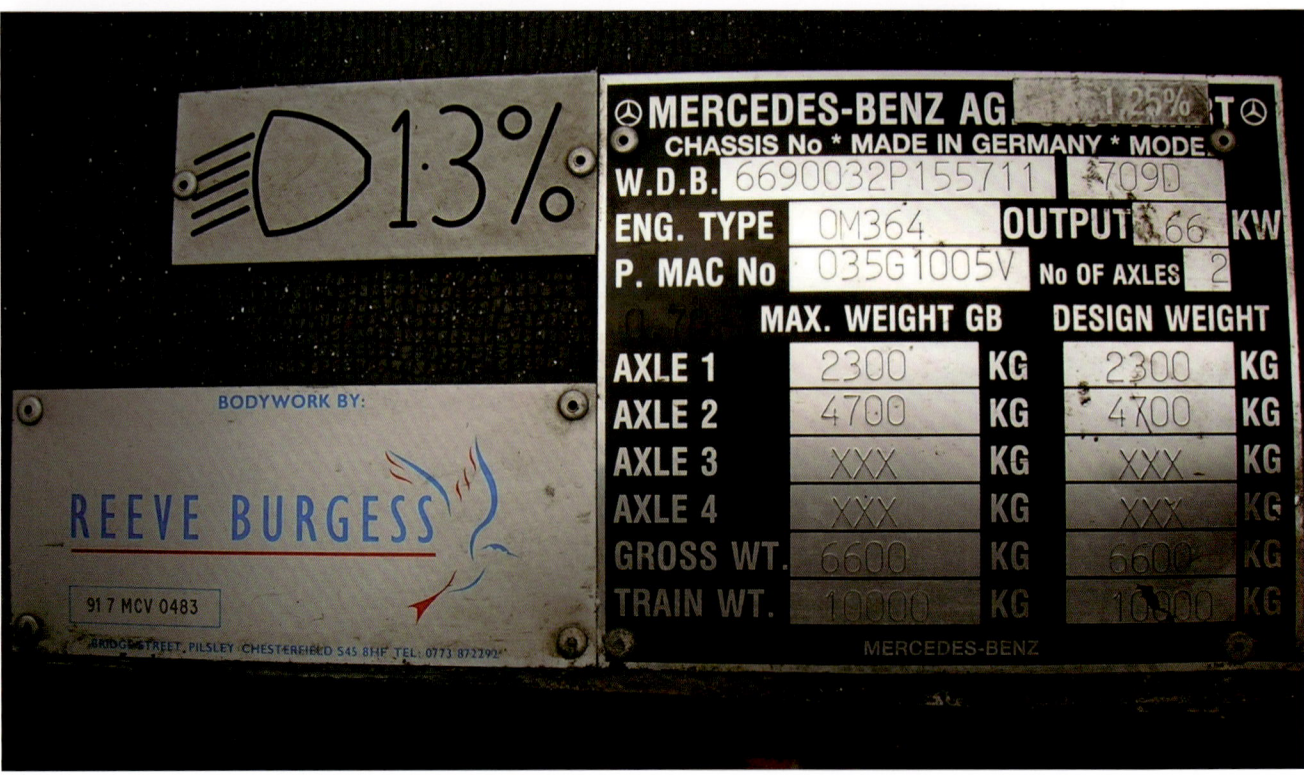

Within a year and by the time J857 FTC was delivered to Badgerline, the maker shown on the chassis plate had been changed from Daimler-Benz AG to Mercedes-Benz AG. Also changed was the Reeve-Burgess body plate, following the company's absorption by Plaxton. Although still quoting the Pilsley company's name and address, the plate now has the Plaxton logo and, more importantly, a body number in the Plaxton series. This number indicates it was built to the 1991 programme and was 7 metres long, the letter M confirming it was mounted on a Mercedes-Benz chassis.

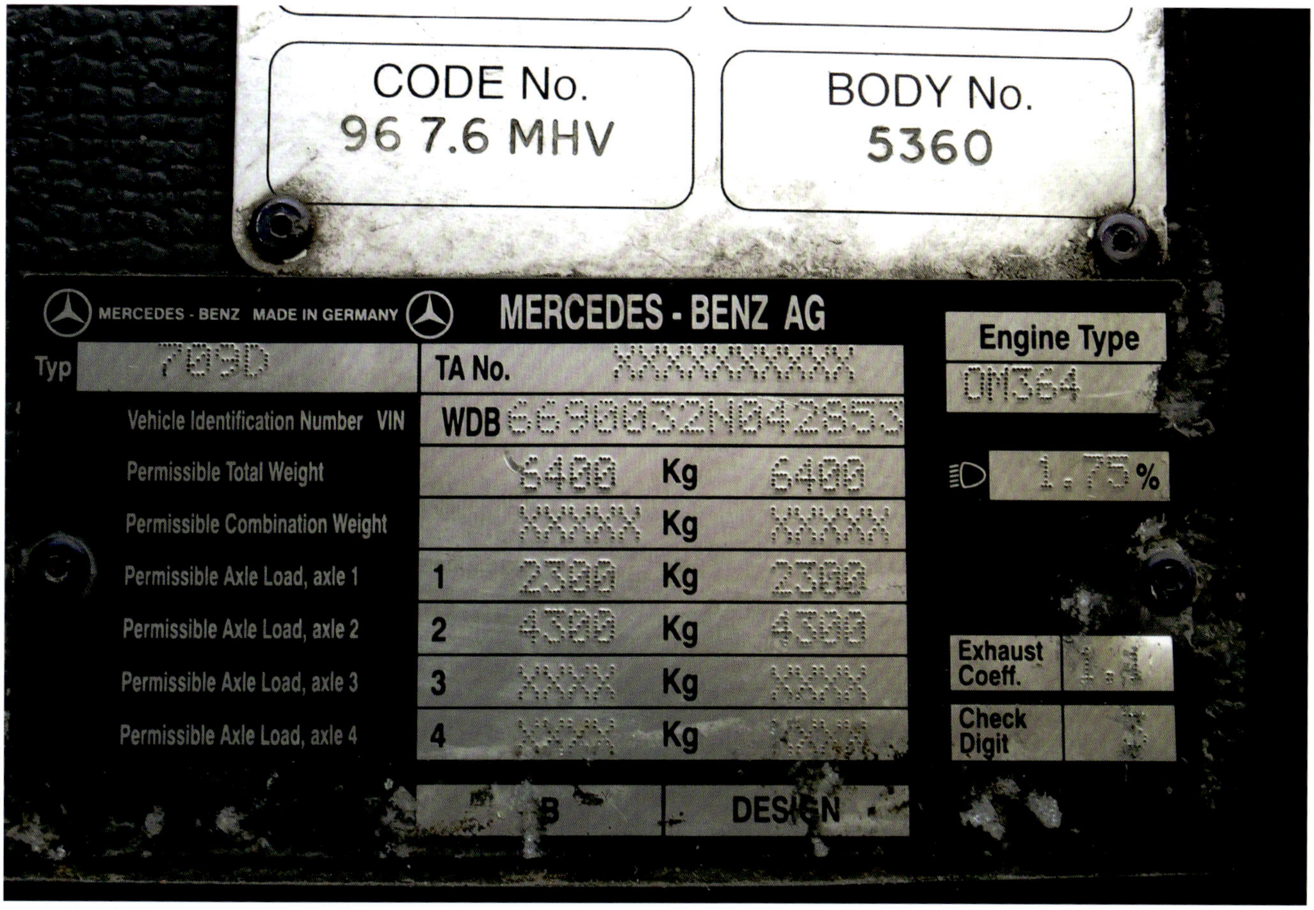

An entirely new style of chassis plate was introduced by 1996, as exemplified by this 709D, with a long tailed, 7.6 metre, Plaxton Beaver body, yet again registered through Luton, being N386 JGS. It was new to Luton & District Transport, but by the time of this photograph, it was running for Dave Fricker's North Somerset Coaches. Strangely, the 'gross weight' of 6600 kilograms shown on the plate of the J-registered bus has been reduced to a 'permissible total weight' of 6400 kg here. The engine's power output is no longer stated.

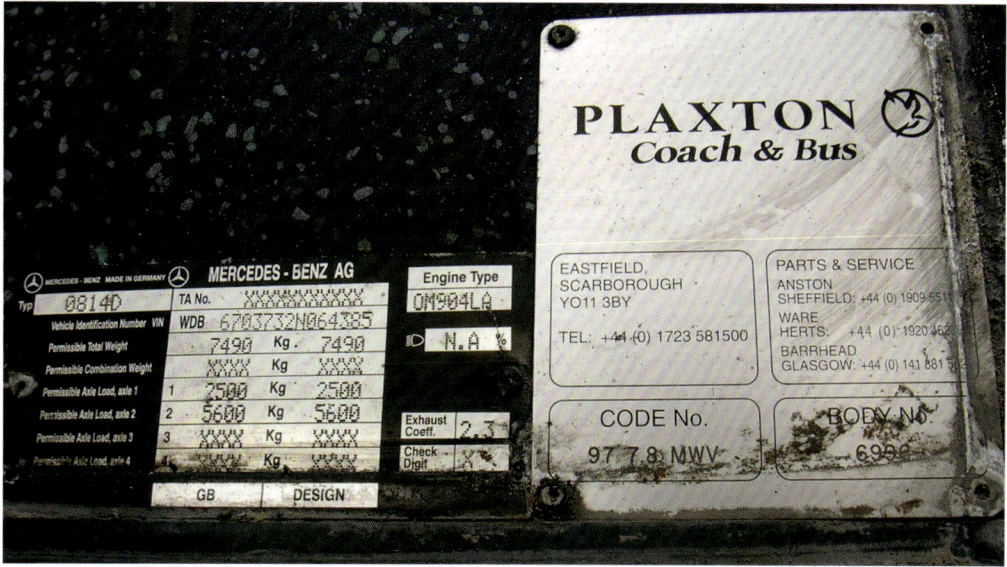

These Mercedes-Benz and Plaxton plates belonged to a similar-sized bus only a year newer, but refer to a Vario O814D, with a short wheelbase (*Baumuster* 670373) and a Beaver 2 body of 7.8 metres in length. This bus was one of a batch built for Eastern Counties, being registered P815 REX.

THE INS AND OUTS • 87

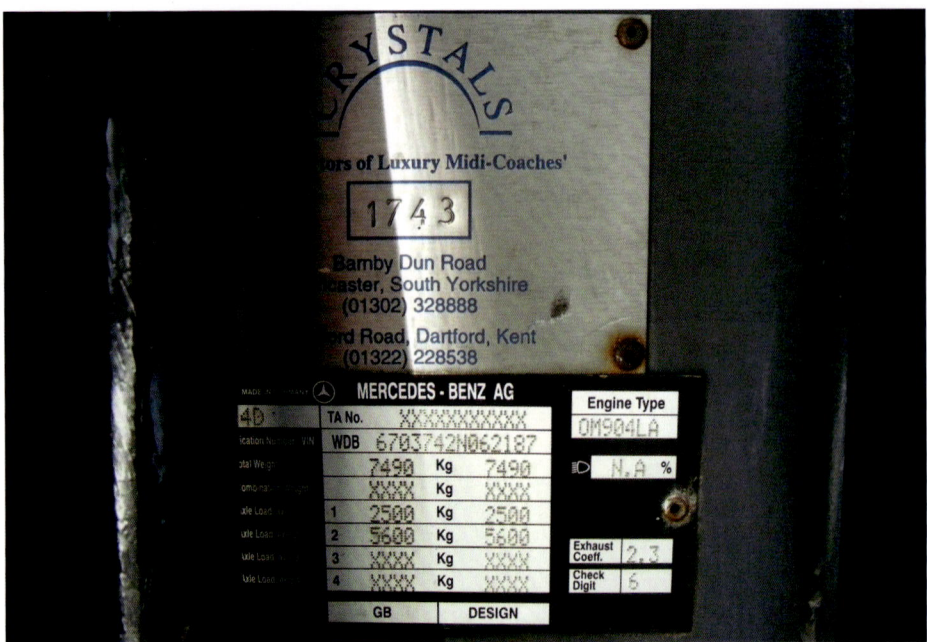

Finally, another Vario, but of the long wheelbase variety (*Baumuster* 670374). Note that the Permissible Total Weight and Axle ratings are the same as on the short wheelbase version. A different make of body is carried on this bus, being by Crystals of Doncaster, to the Whittaker design. It was dealer registered through Peterborough as P652 PFL before delivery to Smith of Coatbridge, although it later became P3 OBS.

A posed publicity photograph, presumably arranged by Reeve-Burgess to show off their new Beaver body. The backdrop is the famous twisted spire of Chesterfield Cathedral, which is not far from the manufacturer's plant at Pilsley. *Author's collection*

SECTION 3

THE MERCEDES-BENZ MIDIBUS IN SOUTH WEST ENGLAND

There should be no doubt that the Mercedes-Benz midibus was put to work in all corners of the British Isles. Each region had its own varied operating conditions and its own range of operators, some of which would be members of large groups (which had their own ideas about the most suitable vehicles for their members' needs), while others would be small, privately-run operators, often experienced in catering for rural communities. The options available just with the Mercedes-Benz T2 were extensive, as we have seen, so that, in any area of the country, it was very likely there would be suitable T2s at work. The buses would offer visual differences by their distinctive and easily recognisable styles of bodywork, which, as Section 1 has shown, came from a host of different builders. There were also the wide-ranging colour-schemes in which they were painted.

For this survey, just one region of the United Kingdom has been chosen, namely the South West of England, though the fleet mix could apply to almost any region. Operating conditions in the South West ranged from the wide-open moorlands of Devon and Cornwall to busy cities like Plymouth, Exeter, Bristol and Gloucester. But there was a Merc T2 to suit them all.

The major operators in this region reached Deregulation Day in October 1986 either still in the ownership of the state, as subsidiaries of the NBC, or, in two cases, run by city/town councils. Until the early 1980s, the whole South West region had been covered by just three NBC companies – Western National Omnibus Company, Hants & Dorset Motor Services and Bristol Omnibus Company. It was significant, though, that the NBC's Regional Director for Western England had instigated the breaking up of the huge companies under his jurisdiction, in the belief that smaller companies had a better understanding of their own operations and would be more economically viable. The first company to be broken up was Midland Red in 1981, as recorded in the paragraphs detailing Carlyle bodywork in Section 1 of this work.

The improved financial returns of the smaller Midland Red concerns encouraged the break-up of the three south-western NBC fleets in 1983. In January, Western National Omnibus Company Ltd was succeeded by Western National Ltd, Southern National Ltd, Devon General Ltd and North Devon Ltd. In the April, Hants & Dorset Motor Services Ltd, which had absorbed Wilts & Dorset Motor Services Ltd around ten years previously, was reformed as Wilts & Dorset Bus Company Ltd and Hampshire Bus Company Ltd, although the operations in eastern Hampshire were merged with those of the Gosport & Fareham Omnibus Company (trading as Provincial). Finally, in the September, Bristol Omnibus Company's northern territory, across to Swindon in Wiltshire, was separated as the Cheltenham & Gloucester Omnibus Company Ltd. Bristol Omnibus Company was further split at the start of 1986, when services outside the city of Bristol were transferred to a new company with a 'trendy' new name – Badgerline Ltd.

In the following fleet analyses, there is a summary of what types of small bus were chosen before the first Mercedes-Benz T2s arrived and how the Mercedes-Benz fleets developed.

MAJOR OPERATORS

WESTERN NATIONAL LTD.
This company's operations covered Cornwall and south-west Devon. Cornwall is characterised by Bodmin Moor and many remote coastal and inland villages, accessed by narrow lanes between high hedges. On the other hand, there are populous and industrialised communities around Camborne-Redruth, St Austell, Penzance and Plymouth. The region is a very popular holiday destination, so in summer, not only do more passengers need to be catered for, but traffic increases immensely, with the associated congestion.

Western National, despite being a member of the National Bus Company, did not take to the Ford Transit minibus. The company went straight to the slightly larger Mercedes-Benz L608D. A fleet of 107 of these was built up between 1984 and 1987, many with 'Hoppa' fleetnames, inferring that these buses could take the public quickly and conveniently to their local destinations. Then, in October 1987, Western National did take a small fleet of Ford Transits. These were unusual in being of the 'sloping-nosed' Mark III model, not commonly used for minibus PSV application. In a little over a year, however, they had all been transferred to Western National's new parent company, Badgerline, to take part in competitive initiatives in Wiltshire and Dorset. Similarly, a 1988 batch of five Iveco 49-10s, which carried the Reeve-Burgess Beaver body, was transferred to Badgerline, in 1992.

In 1990, though, Western National took on a new direction, centred on the large midibus. The company from here on chose the 31-seat Mercedes-Benz 811D. The bodywork chosen initially was the Carlyle C16 model. The first two deliveries were even registered by Carlyle through Birmingham VLO – 301-305 being G151-5 GOL, while 306-311 were H891-6 LOX. The next fifteen buses, however, were registered

Western National's first choice of midibus was the 31-seat 811D, bodied by Carlyle. Here, 322 (H722 HGL) stands at the joint rail and bus stations in St Austell. Western National had quickly discarded NBC leaf-green livery in favour of a harsh blue and white, with coloured bands, as shown in Section 1, but this was soon softened to blue and cream, with one red band. *Graham Jones.*

locally through Truro, 312-326 carrying H712-726 HGL. As was often the case in this size of bus, a few were fitted with coach-type seats, to make them suitable for private hire duties.

Whilst the delivery of 312-326 was taking place, Badgerline sent down four of their 811D-based Optare StarRiders, on loan. Western National numbered these as 327-330. They were E807/8/20/2 MOU, although quickly, E822 MOU was swapped for E812 MOU. Accordingly, Western National adjusted their fleet-numbers, so that 327-330 were now E807/8/12/20 MOU. These four buses were transferred to Western National ownership at the end of the year and they were repainted shortly afterwards.

For a further thirty 811Ds in 1992, the choice of bodywork was changed to the Plaxton Beaver B31F. These were numbered 331-360 (K331-343 OAF, K344-354 ORL and L355-360 VCV). Delivered at the same time were forty-nine 709Ds, with Beaver B23F bodies – 601-625 (K601-625 ORL) and 628-651 (L628-651 VCV). Delivered with the last of these, in 1994, were the first Dennis Darts and no more Mercedes-Benz midibuses were bought new.

It will be seen there was a break in the fleet-numbering sequence of the 709Ds. The numbers 626/7 were allocated in September 1993 when Roselyn Coaches (Ede & Paramour) of Par, Cornwall, withdrew from service work and sold two 709Ds to Western National. 626/7 had less-common bodywork by Wadham-Stringer. The former, registered by the bodybuilder as H825 ERV, seated 27, while the latter was a very short bus, with only 21 seats. It was originally registered J6 EDE but was re-registered J901 MAF when passing to Western National.

In 1995, Western National, in common with other Badgerline Group companies, became part of FirstBus, as explained in more detail later,

Western National's parent concern, Badgerline, lent them four of their ground-breaking Optare StarRider 811Ds in 1991. They were soon purchased and here, at Camborne, is 330 (E820 MOU). It is on the trunk route to Truro. *Graham Jones.*

Seventy-nine more Mercedes-Benz T2s were delivered in 1992-94, but with Plaxton Beaver bodywork. These carried another variant of the livery – returning to blue and white, it was known as the 'Badgers and Flags' scheme, due to the adornments. One of the thirty 811Ds is 348 (K348 ORL), seen on a Plymouth city service.

in the Badgerline section. Western National then started to take in T2s from fellow FirstBus companies, starting in 1996 with two 709D/Beavers from First West Yorkshire. They were numbered to follow the highest current example, as 652/3 (M246/226 VWU). In contrast, 1998 saw the arrival of five somewhat earlier 709D/Beavers, transferred from South Wales Transport (SWT) and Brewers of Maesteg, now 654-8 (E283-6 UCY and E288 VEP). Then, as number 659, came a somewhat newer example, N719 GRV, transferred from Provincial of Fareham.

More noteworthy, however, was the arrival during 1998 of twenty-three of the First Centrewest (London), F-registered 811Ds with Alexander B28F wide-doorway bodies. These were soon upseated to thirty-one. They were numbered in one of several new and seemingly random series, as 5018-5041 (although 5030 was not used), but applied as the buses arrived in a haphazard order. It became known that one reason for obtaining them was to replace the G- and H-registered 811Ds, as the Carlyle bodies on those were in trouble, due to issues with corrosion.

In March 1999, the few batches of buses numbered below 1000 were given 4-figure fleet-numbers. The native 811Ds were altered from the 300s to the 6300s, while similarly, the 709Ds changed from the 600s to the 6600s. The ex-London 811Ds were also renumbered, being placed ahead of existing 811Ds as 6270-81/83-93 in the same untidy order.

Also in March 1999 and in accordance with FirstBus policy, Western National Ltd was renamed First Western National Buses Ltd. The following month, FirstBus purchased two other former Western National Omnibus Company

Above: Another from the same batch of 811Ds is seen a little later in life, not only in yet another livery variation, but carrying 'First' titles and a revised fleet-number of 6344 (K344 ORL). The bus, on the 80 group of routes from Plymouth, is leaving the Torpoint Ferry, having crossed the River Tamar which forms the border between Devon and Cornwall for much of its length.

Below: First Western National took advantage of the availability of some of First London's Alexander-bodied 811Ds. Seen here is 6272 (F677 XMS, formerly MA77), passing through Tregony in Cornwall – a world away from its old London surroundings. *John Young.*

off-shoots, namely Southern National Ltd and North Devon Ltd, which are described under those headings, below. North Devon Ltd, trading as Red Bus, was immediately placed under the wing of First Western National, so re-uniting these divisions. The business was fully absorbed in the June, under the title of First Red Bus Ltd. The occasion also saw that fleet renumbered, to fit it into the latest First Western National series (again, see below). Not long after, the ex-First West Yorkshire 709Ds, 6652/3, were transferred to the Red Bus fleet and repainted, with branding for the Barnstaple Park & Ride being applied to these 25-seaters.

Yet more T2s were transferred in, from late 1999, particularly from First PMT. 6383-5, though, were noteworthy, as these 811Ds had unusual-looking PMT Ami 'full-front' bodies (G337 XRE, H351/3 HRF). Most of the rest were of the familiar 709D/Beaver combination and came from SWT, Capital Citybus and more from PMT, plus several former Bristol City Line and Badgerline examples. By contrast and to add variety, the rare PMT Bursley bodywork was carried by 6666/8 (H481 & 180 JRE), while 6676/7 (L494/5 HRE) carried Dormobile Routemaker 2 bodywork and came in 2002 after a spell with First Bristol.

In 1998, for all its new buses, FirstBus had chosen a new standard livery. This used off-white, relieved by dark-blue and magenta. The use of the latter colour led to it being nicknamed the 'Barbie' livery, as it reminded people of Barbie dolls. For existing buses that were neither low-floor nor finished with the new First pattern of interior trim – and this included all Mercs, of course – a 'Barbie 2' scheme was adopted from 2001. Dark blue was carried on the roof and skirt, with the lower panels receiving a vinyl covering in magenta, which faded from bottom to top, to leave the panels grey at the top.

Also obtained from First London, but new to Eastern National in Essex, was 6382 (F800 RHK), an 811D with Reeve-Burgess Beaver bodywork, finished with the shallow destination screen. The bus is another to be seen at Camborne bus station.

Above: The very uncommon PMT Bursley bodywork is carried by this acquired 709D, 6666 (H481 JRE), seen at Penzance. It was one of two examples transferred from First PMT, whereas most others from that fleet carried Beaver bodies.

Below: In the new FirstBus 'Barbie 2' livery is 6674 (J864 HWS), a 709D-Plaxton Beaver 23-seater, transferred from Badgerline. It is on lay-over from the 87B at the new Truro bus-station, ahead of a native Dennis Dart-Plaxton Pointer on the related 87A.

Having come under FirstBus control, North Devon 'Red Bus' vehicles adopted a 'reversed' version of the then-current Western National livery, with a red skirt and a blue band. One of many Alexander Sprint-bodied 709Ds acquired second-hand by former parent the Cawlett Group, M677 RAJ (new to OK Motor Services of Bishop Auckland) is now carrying its new FirstBus fleet-number, 51377. *Ken Baker.*

The Mercedes-Benz Vario made its appearance in the fleet in 2004, when several six-year-old examples were transferred from First Midland Red West. 52514 (S514 RWP) is seen at Dartmouth Pontoon, on the town service. It wears the prime Barbie livery, but without the willow-leaf emblem.

Next came a nationwide numbering method, using five figures. It was initiated at First PMT in mid-2002 but was appallingly haphazard and lacked any respect to vehicle makes and types. The system had been greatly refined by the time it was applied to First Western National and First Red Bus in January 2004. In this system, Merc T2s for all First fleets in the southern Midlands, the south of England and South Wales were numbered above 50500 and continuing into the 51xxx range. It was based as closely as possible on the buses' registration numbers and age. A table of the numbers applied to FirstBus Mercedes-Benz midibuses in the south-west is given below.

In February 2004, the company was further renamed and, again in accordance with FirstBus policy, it became First Devon & Cornwall Ltd.

Also in early 2004, there was a change in purchasing policy, as the first of nearly thirty S-registered Mercedes-Benz Varios, with Plaxton Beaver 2 bodies, came from First Midland Red Buses Ltd (Midland Red West), who had quickly amassed a fleet of sixty-four such vehicles in 1998. These had followed just six T2s there – and those were 20-seat van conversions – which had joined their fleet of 104 L608Ds, more of which were later acquired second-hand. The Varios had been built as 27-seaters but were made into 22-seaters before being accepted for service in Worcester. With no such restrictions in the south-west, they now ran as 27-seaters.

Another three Varios followed, but these were quite novel, as the bodywork was the Marshall Master. 52591/2/9 (R411/2/9 VPU) came from First Capital in London but were new to Thamesway (Essex Buses Ltd).

PLYMOUTH CITYBUS LTD.

At the time of the deregulation of bus services in October 1986, municipalities that operated buses were required to set up 'arms-length' companies to carry on the operations. Hence the formation of Plymouth Citybus Ltd. The council had already started to protect itself from competition in the deregulated world by ordering no fewer than 81 Dodge or Renault-Dodge S56 midibuses, with Reeve Burgess 23-seat bodywork, for 1986 (adding to four 21-seaters taken early the previous year). These joined a fleet largely composed of double-deck buses.

As early as 1990, though, it was decided to evaluate a replacement model for the Renault/

In 1990, Plymouth Citybus assessed four Mercedes-Benz 709Ds before choosing a midibus with which to replace their 4-year-old fleet of Renault/Dodge S56 23-seaters. The first two 709Ds had uncommon Wadham Stringer Wessex bodywork. This is 202 (H362 BDV), on Royal Parade.

Dodge fleet. Two Mercedes-Benz 709Ds were ordered, with bodywork by Wadham-Stringer and seating 25. They were numbered 201/2 (H361/2 BDV). Two more 709Ds soon followed, as 203/4 (H683/4 BTA), but this time with Reeve-Burgess Beaver B25F bodies. The bodies of all four were of the long tailed variety, so potentially able to seat twenty-nine. At Plymouth Citybus' request, the drivers had their own door on the right-hand side of the cab in all four buses. Furthermore, on the two Beavers, the emergency exit door was a little further forward than normal.

The outcome of the evaluation was that seventy more 709Ds were ordered, all with Beaver long tailed B25F bodies, with drivers' doors. The first ones were badged as Reeve-Burgess products, the rest coming under Plaxton's name. They were numbered 205-274 (J205-225 KTT, K226-247 SFJ, L248-260 YOD and M261-274 HOD).

Left: The other two assessment 709Ds had Reeve-Burgess Beaver bodies which won the day. On 203 (H683 BTA), note the unusual position for the emergency door.

Below: One of the resultant Beaver-bodied 709Ds, 213 (J213 KTT), is seen on Royal Parade being pursued by a Western National Beaver-bodied 811D, 349 (K349 ORL). Despite formerly co-operating over local services, there was now ongoing rivalry between the two operators, so were the layouts of the liveries especially designed to mislead the public?

Plymouth Citybus soon altered their livery to a less dramatic scheme, by changing the lower panels from black and red to red and grey. This is shown by 259 (L259 YOD).

DEVON GENERAL LTD.

It hardly needs to be repeated that Devon General was the company that launched the idea of running high-frequency city services with 16-seat Ford Transits, starting in Exeter in 1984. In 1988, although still taking Ford Transits into stock, thoughts turned to using larger small buses for rural routes in south-east Devon, although again on the basis of replacing full-sized buses more frequently. Two of the then-new Mercedes-Benz 709D model were obtained, carrying Reeve-Burgess Beaver bodies, with 25 coach-like seats, although without head-restraints. They were numbered 50 and 51 (E829/30 ATT) and they had the early style of shallow, full-width destination box. Soon afterwards, a further forty-four similar 'Minicoaches', as Devon General christened them, took up service, numbered 48/9 (F748/9 FDV) and 52-93 (F712-745/756-763 FDV). Interestingly, all had drivers' doors on the offside, so Plymouth Citybus' idea was not new.

Transit Holdings, Devon General's parent organisation, later divided the Devon operations into two, with the services and vehicles in the populous Torbay holiday region now trading under the name of Bayline. The 709Ds remained part of the Devon General fleet.

With the Transit Holdings group in operation in other parts of southern England by 1989, it became quite common for vehicles to be transferred from one fleet to another. For example, a batch of ten similar 709Ds was transferred to Bayline from Thames Transit at Oxford; they retained their numbers 334-343. They had been registered F404-413 KOD through Exeter VLO, as it was standard practice for Transit Holdings to register its buses through Exeter.

Above: Despite its apparent desire to replace all big buses with Ford Transit 16-seaters, Devon General appreciated that longer, rural routes deserved something more accommodating. Two 25-seat Mercedes-Benz 709Ds were taken into stock in 1988, for assessment. They had Reeve-Burgess Beaver bodies. The second of the pair, 51 (E830 ATT), is seen leaving Exeter bus station, to head up to Dartmoor on a route especially chosen for the pair. *Graham Jones*.

Below: The two assessment 709Ds proved their worth, so a batch of forty more was delivered, with further examples being placed with sibling Thames Transit in Oxford. The Devon buses, however, did replace big buses – double-deckers at that – on trunk routes. Twenty-five-seater 53 (F713 FDV) pauses in Exminster, between Exeter and the popular Devon holiday resorts of Dawlish and Teignmouth, on its way to Newton Abbot. *Graham Jones*.

Ten other 709Ds were transferred when still young from Thames Transit to the new Bayline division in south Devon. 337 (F407 KOD) is seen passing through Dawlish on a hot summer's day, on another branch of the 85. *Ken Baker.*

Meanwhile, in 1988, a private operator in Torbay, Burton's of Brixham (Brixham Coaches Ltd) sold out, after stiff competition, to Transit Holdings – in practice, to South Midland. In 1990, eight new Mercedes-Benz 811Ds, with Carlyle B33F bodies, that were part of an order for twelve for the Oxford operations, were diverted to Burton's, with the initial four of the batch soon following them. They retained their numbers 355-366 and, of course, had Exeter registrations – G831-842 UDV.

After the combined Transit Holdings fleets turned in 1993 to the Iveco 59-12, for nearly 100 buses with quaint, dual-doorway Mellor 'Duet' bodywork, Exeter was in receipt in 1995 of twenty-five more Mercedes-Benz 709Ds. These, like the Ivecos, had the dual-doorway layout, which made them unique. Their Marshall C19 bodies thus seated B21D. They received fleetnumbers after the latest B21D Ivecos, as 1034-1058. Their registrations were obtained through Luton VLO, because of the dealership that had agreed to handle the order, so were M226-250 UTM.

In February 1996, in a surprising move, Transit Holdings sold their Devon operations to the Stagecoach group. The history of Stagecoach since it was created in 1980 has been well documented. Its expansion was rapid, through the acquisition of National Bus Company subsidiaries and Scottish Bus Group operators, followed by the purchase of several such operators that had already been privatised, such as the Cheltenham & Gloucester group, detailed below. Now

THE MERCEDES-BENZ MIDIBUS IN SOUTH WEST ENGLAND • 101

Above: Intended for the Oxford operations of Transit Holdings, a batch of 33-seat Mercedes 811Ds, with Carlyle bodies, was placed with the newly-acquired Burtons of Brixham operation. Seen on Torquay seafront is 363 (G839 UDV). The banner at the top of the windscreen states Riviera Connection. *Ken Baker.*

Below: This bus presents a unique appearance – a T2 with dual-doorway bodywork. From 1993, Transit Holdings standardised on dual-doorway Mellor bodywork for its Iveco midibuses, so when returning to the Mercedes-Benz, it was logical that their Marshall bodies should also have two doors. Now renumbered 463, M245 UTM carries one of the 'Exeter Minibus' colour-schemes. *Graham Jones.*

the Transit Holdings companies were added. Stagecoach not only had its own favoured types of new bus, but – controversially – it had also decided to impose its own distinctive livery upon all its subsidiaries. This was white, with bold stripes in orange, red and blue – nicknamed, of course, 'toothpaste stripes', due to the similarity to a certain brand of toothpaste. Stagecoach was not a supporter of Devon's widespread use of 16-seat minibuses so the group's standard choice of midibus quickly made its appearance, in what was now called the Stagecoach Devon fleets. Eighteen brand new examples were diverted from other Stagecoach companies. The model was the Mercedes-Benz 709D, bearing Alexander Sprint bodywork, featuring only a single doorway, of course.

Their delivery coincided with a renumbering of the Devon fleets in March 1996, in which Merc 709Ds were placed in the 400s. The new intake was therefore numbered 470-487. Numbers 470-474 were diverted from Stagecoach companies in the south-east of England and were registered through Brighton as N978-982 NAP. The next thirteen were from a batch of fifteen intended for Ribble, who must have felt hard done by. Therefore 475-487 were registered through Manchester as N506-518 BJA.

Later, a number of earlier Mercs was transferred in from other Stagecoach fleets. Acquisitions started in a surprising way, with eighteen 709D-Reeve-Burgess van-conversion 20-seaters, from Newcastle Busways (now 488-505). They included several of the first, groundbreaking, batch that were mentioned in Section 1, with D-TFT registrations. Also coming were ten London-pattern Alexander-bodied 811Ds from the F-XMS series, which had latterly been in the

Once Stagecoach had acquired the Devon fleets in 1996, their standard choice of midibus, carrying the infamous 'toothpaste-stripes' livery, started to replace the Ford Transits. Eighteen new Mercedes-Benz 709Ds, with Alexander Sprint bodies, were diverted to Devon from other Stagecoach fleets. One of thirteen intended for Ribble was N509 BJA, now numbered 478. It is seen on Torquay Strand on a town service. *Ken Baker.*

Transferred within the Stagecoach empire from London were ten wide-doorway 811D 28-seaters. No.594 (F616 XMS, previously MA16) stands in Exeter ready for its next trip to Sandy Bay, via Exmouth. *Ken Baker.*

Stagecoach East London or Selkent divisions. As they arrived, they were numbered downwards from 598 – interestingly, twenty-three sister buses, that had become FirstBus possessions with two other London fleets, later came west as well, in this case to Western National.

Deserving special mention is the bus that carried the number 599; this vehicle, H889 NFS, was an 814D coach, bearing stark-looking PMT Ami bodywork. It came from Stagecoach Bluebird in northern Scotland but was one of a small batch of similar vehicles that had been supplied new to Scottish small operators.

Once production of the Mercedes T2 had been discontinued in 1997, Stagecoach as a group ordered only a relatively small number of the successor model, the Vario. However, Stagecoach Devon was one of the operators that received a batch. Sixteen arrived in mid-1998. Due to certain registration numbers being withheld for sale by the DVLA, the Varios were numbered 101-105, 107-110 and 112-118 (R101 through to R116 NTA, S117/8 JFJ). These again had Alexander bodywork, but of the ALX100 design, in its 'Mark II' form. Seating was for just 25, despite their length.

The transfer of 'mid-life' Merc T2s from other Stagecoach fleets resumed in 1998, with 506-511 (N201-6 CUD) from established sister company Thames Transit in Oxford. These, however, were 711Ds, with Marshall bodies, so were not dissimilar in looks to native buses 444-468 (M226-250 UTM) – other than not having two doorways.

By 1999, the ex-Newcastle van-conversions had gone (also being withdrawn now were the F-FDV 'minicoaches'), so when three

Above: Stagecoach Devon was one of the select number of fleets in the group to receive a batch of the new Mercedes-Benz Vario model. Sixteen were delivered in 1998 and this is 103 (R103 NTA) in Exeter High Street. It was photographed after being repainted into the later and very different form of livery, launched in 2001.

Below: Also in 1998, six three-year-old Mercs, of the 711D model and with Marshall bodies, were transferred from Stagecoach Thames Transit. Here, 508 (N203 CUD) passes through Dawlish. Since the photo above was taken at this spot, showing 337 (F407 KOD), there have been several changes, including a considerable expansion of Bailey's Fish and Chip restaurant. *John Young*.

Stagecoach-standard Alexander Sprint-709Ds were transferred from Red & White, they re-utilised the numbers 488-490 (L685 CDD, M345/60 JBO); the first had been new to Cheltenham & Gloucester. The sequence was continued from late-2000, when nine similar buses came directly from Cheltenham & Gloucester, but by clever planning, the numbers 491-499 were matched to registrations L691-6 CDD and M697-9 EDD. The next seven in the series followed – M701-5 EDD and M706/7 JDG – but these were given the numbers 401-407. Other specimens were to follow.

In 2001, a new pattern of Stagecoach livery started to replace the famous 'toothpaste stripes'. Still using a white base, the front end now carried two shades of blue, while the rear end was all-red, each area being separated from the white by orange swoops.

The dual-doorway bodywork of the Iveco 59-12s had not found favour with Stagecoach management and a programme had run to convert them to single-doorway. During 2002, the policy was extended to the dual-doorway Mercs, 444-468, which thereafter seated B23F.

In January 2003, the entire Stagecoach stock across Great Britain was renumbered into a single series, using five figures. This scheme was much tidier and more carefully planned than the series that had been inaugurated by FirstBus six months earlier. Mercedes-Benz 709Ds were renumbered into the 40000s, based upon the registration numerals as often as possible, so that M226-250 UTM (now the oldest in stock in Devon) became 40226-40250. In the same way, the 1996 Stagecoach-standard diversions became 40506-518 and 40978-982, thereby keeping registration batches together across the Group's fleets. Ex-Red & White M345/60 JBO, however, needed to become 40545/560 (further examples came from this batch later), but ex-C&GOC L685/91-6 CDD, et seq, became 40685/691-6 and so on.

Stagecoach Devon's Mercedes Varios, R101 NTA, etc., were re-numbered 42101 upwards.

SOUTHERN NATIONAL LTD AND NORTH DEVON LTD.

This pair of companies had one of the most varied fleets of Mercedes-Benz T2 midibuses delivered new to any south-western operator. Later, astute second-hand acquisitions were made.

Neither Southern National Ltd, covering west Dorset and south and west Somerset, nor North Devon Ltd (which traded as Red Bus) had the benefit of working in what could be described as good 'bus territory'. Their operations covered mainly rural, agricultural land, with Exmoor protruding into North Devon's area. There were, for all that, pockets of higher population, including Weymouth, Yeovil, Taunton, Ilfracombe, Barnstaple and Bideford. Once again, the two areas see a huge influx of summer tourists. The less than sparkling trading figures of the companies ensured the two stayed unsold by the NBC until well after 1986. In the end, the managements of both firms set up a holding company, Cawlett Ltd, to acquire the two operators from the NBC, this taking place in March 1988.

It is probably not surprising that under the NBC, the Ford Transit was seen as an ideal tool to improve finances. Southern National took just short of 100 and North Devon received nearly fifty. Soon afterwards, North Devon took just three Iveco 49-10 21-seaters and that led them to seek out several low-mileage used examples of this model.

In 1991, things began to change. Cawlett developed a programme of ordering batches of rather higher capacity midibuses, on Mercedes-Benz T2 chassis. There were two distinct types of bus, which were numbered separately in their combined fleet numbering system – 709Ds with long tailed 29-seat bodies, or 811Ds with 33 seats. Physically, of course, there was not a lot of difference between the two types.

The first batch of ten buses, on 709D chassis, was originally shared by Southern National (701-706) and North Devon (707-710), although, after only one month, 707/8/10 were transferred to Southern National. The batch was registered through Taunton as H906-910/912-6 WYB (the number 911 tended to be withheld by the DVLA for hopeful sale – at a premium – to purchasers of a certain model of Porsche sports car). The bodywork chosen was the Carlyle C19. Cawlett had introduced a new livery for its small buses, of yellow, with two bands at waist-level – the bands were different colours for the three different divisions, Dorset, Somerset and North Devon. The yellow North Devon buses still persisted in displaying the fleet-name of Red Bus.

For their second batch of 709D 29-seaters, Cawlett chose Wright Nimbus bodywork, which was rather softer in appearance than the Carlyle design. Possibly, all were intended for the Dorset area, as the registrations were obtained from Bournemouth VLO – 711-718 were J140-6/8 SJT (appropriately, JT was a former Dorset index mark). In the event, 712/7/8 were placed with Red Bus at Barnstaple.

The batch was quickly followed by further examples carrying the Carlyle design, although these bodies were completed by Marshall, following Carlyle's collapse. Shared by three Somerset depots, the four were registered through Taunton one at a time, as the registration year would be drawing to a close at the end of July 1992. So, 719-722 were J969 EYD, and J241, 580 and 601 FYA. No.722 had the final body attributed to Carlyle.

At the same time, North Devon received the group's first 33-seat 811D. It also had Carlyle-Marshall bodywork, but started a separate numbering series, at 750. This branch obtained the registration through Exeter, this being J610 PTA. It was not painted yellow but was red below the waist and white above.

It was joined at the end of 1992 by a further single 811D, 751. This time, a matching Exeter registration was obtained, K751 VFJ. The choice

Newly in service in April 1991 in Southern National's Somerset division with dual-green waist-bands are 701/5 (H906/10 WYB), from their first batch of long tailed 29-seat 709Ds. The bodywork is the Carlyle C19. Taunton bus station's parking bays provide the attractive setting. *Graham Jones.*

Above: For the Cawlett Group's second batch of Mercs, the bodywork chosen was the rather more-rounded Wright Nimbus. Yellow Red Bus 718 (J148 SJT) is seen at the Exeter on-street starting point of route 359 up to Dartmoor, the contract having been won from Devon General – see above. *Graham Jones.*

Below: The first 33-seat 811D for the Cawlett Group was 750 (J610 PTA), for which the body order went back to Carlyle. The bus was allocated to North Devon Ltd but was the only Merc to carry this red and white livery. It is seen on Bideford Quay, carrying South Western fleetnames for the contracted services based on Exeter. It has just passed a Red Bus Ford Transit minibus. *Ken Baker.*

of bodywork on this yellow bus swung back to the Wright Nimbus, which was also specified for the 1993 deliveries. Firstly, there came a sole 709D 29-seater, for North Devon's contracted network trading as Tiverton & District. The bus was 723 (K723 WTT). For the Red Bus area were more 33-seat 811Ds, 752-755 (K752-5 XTA).

The end of 1993 saw another mixed bag. Southern National received a sole 29-seat 709D, 724, which was again Wright-bodied. A significant improvement to the bodywork was that the pillars had been re-aligned to produce three even-sized windows on the offside. Weymouth-based 724 was registered through Bournemouth as L649 CJT. Weymouth also received three 811D 33-seat versions, 756-758 (L650-2 CJT), while for the Somerset division were 759 and 760 (L329/30 MYC). A further three for Dorset arrived in the summer of 1994 – 761-763 (L67-69 EPR – another former Dorset index).

The following month saw six 811Ds arrive with North Devon, but with Marshall bodies once again. The batch was 764-769, again with matching Exeter marks, M764-9 FTT. The first three carried a special livery of light-blue and white, with the fleetname Atlantic Blue. This was an operation set up in Ilfracombe to combat competition from the local Filers business. The three yellow examples, meanwhile, were equipped with coach seats.

All-white paintwork was carried by the next delivery, but the bus was intended for assessment. It was a 709D, so was numbered 725, but, for a change, it carried Alexander (Belfast) Sprint B29F bodywork. It had an Edinburgh registration, M305 TSF. It seemed to make an impression, because over the next few months came ten more Alexander Sprint 709Ds. These, though, were built at Falkirk. Somerset-based 726-735 had a miscellany of registrations – M802-5 UYA, M278/9/81/2 UYD and M239/40 VYA. Old ties had not been forgotten, though, as 811Ds 770-773 (M241/2 & 508/9 VYA), which were also allocated to Somerset depots, once again carried

As Filers of Ilfracombe were using blue and white buses to compete against Red Bus on the trunk route to Westward Ho., Red Bus introduced blue and white buses on *their* route. Three new blue and white Marshall-bodied 811Ds joined in, complete with Atlantic Blue fleetnames. No.764 (M764 FTT) is shown here, having just arrived in Ilfracombe.

Wright Nimbus bodywork. After several months of service, it was noticed that there had been an administrative error and the registrations of 726-9 had to be re-arranged, as M804/3/5/2 UYA (as if the registrations of Cawlett's Mercs were not haphazard enough already).

The year 1995 also saw the purchase of two surprising T2s, which were numbered 901 and 902 (M901/2 LTT). They were 609Ds, with just 19 seats, in van-conversion bodies made by Frank Guy, a business that had developed in this field rather late on in the T2's life. The buses were placed at the Holsworthy outstation in North Devon, to work on service 85 (Bideford-Stibbs Cross-Holsworthy and on down to Launceston in Cornwall).

At about the same time, Cawlett started seeking out suitable used 29- or 33-seat T2s. The first to arrive was an 811D, so it was numbered 774. It was six years old (F154 RHK), but the most remarkable point about this bus was that it was the first Merc in the Cawlett Group to carry what could almost be regarded as the 'standard' bodywork for the T2 – the Beaver body. Being an early example, it was built by Reeve-Burgess and it had the shallow, full-width destination box. The bus had been new to Hedingham & District, but came from Jackson of Bicknacre, also in Essex.

Merc 709Ds 736/7 were former demonstrators, both with Alexander bodywork, being M220 PMS, bodied at Falkirk, and TDZ 3265, bodied by Alexander (Belfast) at Mallusk, so registered through Ballymena.

More new buses of this combination were 738-742 (N556-9/61 EYB). A varied batch of used Alexander-709Ds (some only 25-seaters) took the fleetnumbers up to 749, which abutted the first of the 811Ds, of course. Therefore, further acquired 709Ds were numbered from 950. Meanwhile, more new buses at the end of 1996 were allocated numbers 'the other side' of the 811Ds, as 780-785 (P442/3/5-8 KYC – again a broken sequence of registration-numbers). These Alexander-bodied buses were of special note by being on 711D

In 1995, the Cawlett Group started acquiring Mercs second-hand. The first to arrive was a six-year-old 811D, which, remarkably, became the first Merc in a Cawlett fleet to carry the popular Beaver body. It was numbered 774 (F154 RHK) – First Western National also bought second-hand Beaver-bodied 811Ds with F-RHK registrations, as shown above.

Above: Completed by Alexander (Belfast) at Mallusk as a demonstrator, this 29-seat 709D was registered through Ballymena, as TDZ 3265. After seven months, it was bought by North Devon Ltd, as 737. In a further seven months, it was transferred to Southern National and is seen here after working from Taunton to Wells. In 2001, the registration-number was chosen to disguise the age of a coach, so 737 received a new Bristol mark, N46 OAE.

Below: Built towards the end of the Mercedes-Benz T2 production run, Southern National's 786-790 were noteworthy, not only by being 711Ds, but by being the only Mercs delivered new to Cawlett ever to carry the Beaver coachwork. Seen in Taunton bus-station on a town service is 789 (P182 LYB).

chassis, as Mercedes-Benz was now putting more emphasis on the higher-powered, Euro2 versions of the T2.

Even more notable were the buses that followed them in March 1997, 786-790 (P179-183 LYB), because these were not only 711Ds, but the bodywork was the Plaxton Beaver. They were the only Beaver bodies ever bought new by the Cawlett Group. Seating was for only 25, as the bodies were not of the long tailed variety.

From late 1997, the Cawlett Group continued with the purchase of new Mercedes-Benz midibuses, but in so doing, Southern National and North Devon became the only major operators in the region, besides Stagecoach Devon with its one small batch, to turn to the new Mercedes-Benz Vario. These had Plaxton Beaver 2 bodies. They were on the short wheelbase chassis, so had seating for 27 or 29. The first four went to North Devon, between August 1997 and March 1998. They started another new numbering series, 850-853, and were registered on completion as R650 TDV, R851 YDV and R852/3 TFJ.

In the latter month, the Dorset area received 854-861 (R501-8 NPR). But the interesting aspect about these was that they carried a livery of white and grey, with an orange stripe, and the fleetname of Dorset Transit. This was a trading name of Dorchester Coachways (West Dorset Coaches Ltd), a firm the Cawlett Group had set up to take over the main part of the business of the famous Bere Regis & District. Dorchester Coachways was now being used in a questionable way – to circumvent a ban imposed by the Traffic Commissioner on Southern National, which prevented them from operating the trunk Weymouth to Portland service. This followed severe competition with a small operator, Weybus, which included the blocking of buses at stops and physical aggression. The ban only affected Southern National and there was nothing in the law to prevent another division of Cawlett running the service. Ten of Southern National's Carlyle-bodied 709Ds were also transferred to Dorset Transit and repainted, to add visible strength to the operation.

After T2 production ended, the Cawlett Group continued to buy new Mercs, which of course were Varios. These carried Plaxton Beaver 2 bodies and before long, twenty-three were in service. The first batch for Weymouth wore a white, grey and orange livery and initially worked under the name Dorset Transit, as explained in the text. 858 (R505 NPR) is seen here.

Interesting acquisitions later in 1998 were of eight of Plymouth Citybus' Reeve-Burgess Beaver 709Ds. Numbers 960/5 were H683/4 BTA, while 961-4/6/7 were J208/20/17/05/13/10 KTT – why put them in order when the rest of the fleet was so random?

In late 1998, further new Vario/Beaver 2 buses arrived, 862 in Somerset (S340 WYB) and 863/4 in Dorset (with matching registrations this time, S863/4 LRU). North Devon next received eight more examples, 865-872 (S865-872 NOD). Interestingly, 865 alone was on a long wheelbase chassis, so had 33 seats. With the low-floor Dennis Dart now available, priority was given to purchasing a fleet of these buses, so no more Mercs were ordered after these twenty-three Varios.

In April 1999, the Cawlett Group accepted an offer of purchase from FirstBus. An immediate effect was that, for convenience, Southern National was placed under the control of First Bristol Buses (formerly Bristol Omnibus Company) and received their legal lettering and address on the sides, while similarly, North Devon was placed under the wing of First Western National. This was followed in the June by the absorption of North Devon into First Western National and the application of new fleet-numbers in the Western National series, as follows:

> Nos.6370-80 to the 811Ds, formerly 750/2-5, 763-5/7-9;
> Nos.6520-4/6-30 to 709Ds 711-8, 723/4;
> Nos.6700-11 to the Varios 850-3 and 865-72 (Western National had no Varios of their own).
> The two 609D van-conversions, 901/2, took the numbers 6531/2, while the remaining second-hand 709Ds, 955-7, became 6533-5.

The choice of the new numbers ignored any relationship between the existing fleet- and registration-numbers. It will be noticed that some interfleet transfers between Southern National and North Devon had taken place since the buses were new.

Meanwhile, Southern National buses, including midibuses now, started to be repainted into a new version of the latest livery carried by First

When Plymouth Citybus started to sell off its first 709Ds after only eight years, Southern National snapped up eight of them. J220 KTT became 962 and is seen at Taunton.

Above: In October 2001, Southern National started a new Somerset County Council contract for a local service in Wells in Badgerline territory. The peculiar point was that it was run with a bus from Weymouth. The scheduling was worked in with student services that commenced in Dorset. Vario 864 (S864 LRU) is seen at Wells bus station. The 660 did not survive long and the 29 was diverted to absorb it.

Below: FirstBus acquired the Cawlett Group in 1999 and Southern National was placed under the wing of First Bristol Buses. Repaints then started using a version of the latest Badgerline livery but using Badgerline green between Southern National cream at either end. This is shown by 722 (J601 FYA) at Weymouth. This bus carries the last body attributed to Carlyle, although it was completed by Marshall. Beyond, 720 (J241 FYA) carries overall advertising for Waterside Holiday Park.

Providing strong contrasts at Taunton, despite both being on 1995/96 709D chassis, are ex-Bristol City Line 7904 (N904 HWS), with Plaxton Beaver bodywork and in the new Badgerline-inspired livery, and 742 (N561 EYB), with Alexander Sprint bodywork and in its original Southern National colours.

Bristol's Badgerline division. The new colours were applied diagonally, using Badgerline's bright green between Southern National's cream at either end.

In time, several Mercs were transferred between the Bristol and Southern National fleets (but were not given new numbers) and even from First fleets further afield. Among the latter – making a rather surprising choice – were several N-registered 609D van-conversions, from First Eastern Counties.

Southern National adopted the FirstBus 'Barbie 2' livery for repaints in 2001 (as described under the Western National heading, above), while the company regained some autonomy in April 2001, by becoming First Southern National Ltd. In June 2003, however, the First Southern National operations were divided and merged with those of their neighbouring FirstBus concerns. The Dorset area became part of the new First Hampshire & Dorset, while the Somerset area was merged with First Bristol, which was

Once both areas were under the control of First Somerset & Avon, six of Southern National's Wright Nimbus 811Ds were moved up into former Badgerline territory. 757/8 (L651/2 CJT) are seen here on Weston-super-Mare town services.

Above: From 2001, the FirstBus 'Barbie 2' livery was adopted for repaints. No.971 (N583 WND), a 709D-Alexander (Belfast) Sprint, which was new to Dodds of Troon, stands at the Somerwest World holiday resort at Minehead, Somerset.

Below: Changes to the regulations covering driver training buses decreed that the vehicle had to be no less than 10 metres long. To achieve the new length, First Somerset & Avon fabricated extensions to some of the former Badgerline Optare StarRider driver-trainers, to move the front and rear 'bumpers' outward by about 800m each. The modifications can be seen on Taunton's E803 MOU.

then renamed First Somerset & Avon. The fleet was renumbered in 2004 into First's National scheme, as outlined under the Western National heading.

BADGERLINE LTD.

Badgerline was the first major operator in the south-west to show support for the Mercedes-Benz T2, by ordering two dozen Optare StarRiders almost off the drawing-board. They were based, of course, on the new long wheelbase 811D variant. It was to become the first large batch of StarRiders to be built and Badgerline had co-operated with Optare over certain aspects of their design. Deliveries came in the wake of a demonstration StarRider (E95 RWR) that was tried in late 1987. The new fleet entered service from May 1988. Badgerline regarded these 31-seaters as 'big buses' and certainly not minibuses, so they were delivered in the same livery as used on full-sized buses, with yellow fronts and rears and bright green in the middle, applied with a forward-leaning slope. Minibuses were white, with two bands in yellow and green, plus Minilink names. Furthermore, the StarRiders had fleetnumbers amid other recent single-deckers – 3800-3823 (E800-823 MOU; Badgerline registered its buses through Bristol VLO). Numbers 3819-23 were fitted out with 27 coach seats.

Unfortunately, some technical aspects of the new StarRiders were found to be troublesome in their early days and a lot of warrantee work had to be carried out. To cover failed buses, Optare supplied StarRiders from their own stock of silver-and-blue or plain white float or demonstration vehicles. Several appeared with Badgerline for spells of service.

Badgerline had amassed 138 Ford Transit 16-seaters in 1985/6. These were soon joined by twenty-one Freight-Rover Sherpas, then by forty-four Iveco 49-10s, with Robin Hood City Nipper 19-seat bodies. In 1991, however, a start was made at replacing the Transits (the Sherpas had already gone). The choice fell to the Mercedes-Benz 709D, for which Reeve-Burgess was to supply 23-seat

Badgerline's ground-breaking fleet of two-dozen Optare StarRiders took up service from May 1988. Their duties included working contracted Bristol city services, on behalf of Avon County Council. Seen here in Sylvan Way, Sea Mills, when only three weeks old, is 3804 (E804 MOU).

Beaver bodies; in these, two seats were forsaken for a luggage pen aft of the doorway. The bodies were allocated numbers in the Plaxton series. Ten buses were delivered initially, for the direct replacement of ten Transits on Weston-super-Mare town services. Again, neither did they carry Minilink livery, nor were their fleet-numbers in the minibus series. They were in a new paint scheme of all-over Badgerline green, enhanced by a huge grinning Badger emblem. Their numbers were in an extension of the StarRider series, in being 3850-3859 (J850-9 FTC). Over the next 18 months, the rest of Weston's Transits were seen off by 3860-3866 (J860-6 HWS) and 3867-76 (K867-76 NEU), all with Plaxton Beaver B23F bodies.

After Weston's Transits had been consigned to history, it was the turn for Bath's Transits to be replaced. Firstly, though, an interesting one-off development vehicle was delivered. 3877 (L877 TFB) was a 711D, as described in Section 1 of this book, and it entered service in Bath in November 1993.

Bath then received all thirty-two of 1994's standard 709Ds. Due to certain numbers being withheld by the registration authority for sale to the public, two fleet-numbers were left vacant, so the batch was 3878-87/89-99 and 3901-11 (L878 VHT, etc. – but note that the number 911 was available this time, unlike in Southern National's case). Number 3882 developed a serious fault while on delivery and had to return to Mercedes-Benz for rectification; this resulted in its L-registration being voided and replaced by M882 BEU. Although a small number of Transits remained in the fleet, no more Mercedes-Benz T2s were bought new.

When the Optare StarRiders came to be repainted, they received this all-over green livery.

In April 1994, Badgerline acquired the services of Clapton Coaches of Clapton, near Midsomer Norton, south-west of Bath, with five of their midibuses. Clapton Coaches had only a small fleet, but the Merc T2 had become the standard choice. These buses, though, were of a variety

For its fleet to replace Ford Transit minibuses from 1991, Badgerline standardised on the Reeve-Burgess/Plaxton Beaver-bodied 709D. The first twenty-seven were placed at Weston-super-Mare, where 3873 (K873 NEU) shows off their all-green livery and the huge, smiling, badger emblem.

of layouts. One stipulation by Clapton's owner Maurice Chivers was that the registration numbers should end with a zero. The T2s acquired by Badgerline were –

- E930 YAM, an uncommon 16-seat 507D, new in 1987 with a Reeve-Burgess conversion from a van shell – it is shown in Section 1. Badgerline did not operate this bus.
- E350 AMR (also a Swindon mark) was a 1988 609D which, fairly typically for this model at the time, carried Reeve-Burgess' coach-built Beaver bodywork, with 25 coach seats. This was numbered by Badgerline to follow the new 709Ds, as 3912.
- F850 TCW was a van-conversion 609D 20-seater, again from Reeve-Burgess, which Badgerline numbered 3913. After a while, it was repainted as a (very small) over-all advertisement.
- J850 OBV was a 709D with Plaxton Beaver B23F bodywork, very much in keeping with the Badgerline fleet, and now numbered 3914. The Preston registrations of 3913/4 was due to these two having been supplied by Ciceley Commercials of Blackburn.
- L390 UHU, locally registered this time, was only six-months old and was another 709D/ Beaver 23-seater. It became Badgerline's 3915.

There was one more T2 that came from Clapton. Also fitting in with the Badgerline fleet, it was an Optare StarRider. F695 AWW, registered by Optare through Leeds, was accordingly numbered 3824.

There was one way in which the Clapton Mercs did not comply to Badgerline standards and that was the fitment of automatic gearboxes.

Later in 1994, in October, the Badgerline Group acquired the operations of Roger Durbin of Almondsbury, north of Bristol, and formed Durbin Coaches Ltd to carry on the business, under Bristol Omnibus control. There were two Mercedes-Benz PSVs in the Durbin fleet, an

Badgerline's acquisition of the services and vehicles of Clapton Coaches added some variety to their Mercedes-Benz fleet. No.3912 (E350 AMR) was an early 609D, with Reeve-Burgess Beaver 25-seat bodywork to coach standards, although with a folding door. It is seen here in Bath.

L608D and a 609D van conversion. They were numbered 8944 (D144 NDT) and, for convenience, 8945 (E694 UND). The latter went on to serve the Bristol group, in various divisions, for another 10 years.

Next, in December, agreement was reached with Tim Jennings of Somerbus, which was based in Paulton, again near Midsomer Norton, to end some rivalry. As part of the deal, Badgerline bought two midibuses from Somerbus. One was a Renault-Dodge S56 (which Badgerline did not really want and soon got rid of), but the other was a very smart, 15-month-old Mercedes 709D, K29 OEU. Now numbered 3916, it stood out among Badgerline's other Mercs because it had long tailed, 29-seat, Wright Nimbus bodywork.

Badgerline had adopted an expansionist policy following privatisation in 1986, by setting up competing networks in Wiltshire and Dorset, or, after they had been abandoned, by buying into other former NBC fleets, such as Western National, as mentioned above. In 1995, the successful and now widespread Badgerline Group agreed to merge with Aberdeen-based GRT Holdings, itself also now widespread. The outcome was the creation of FirstBus. There was no change to be seen for a while, but then it was decided that, on 1 January 1996, the management of Badgerline Ltd should be taken over by Bristol Omnibus Company Ltd, from whom it had been split exactly ten years previously. Badgerline, however, was to be retained as a separate division from Bristol's CityLine operations, although the transfer of buses from one to the other, including 709Ds, did occur on occasion.

Later in 1996, ex-Clapton Coaches 609D/ Beaver 3912 (E350 AMR) was transferred to fellow FirstBus company Provincial (Gosport & Fareham Omnibus Company), as number 100. This bus then became a 'guinea pig'. The engine remained in place, but the transmission was stripped out, while an electric motor and special batteries were installed. It was being converted to hybrid diesel-electric drive, whereby the engine at mid-revs would power the electric motor, which, in built-up urban centres, would propel

Another Merc acquired from a local small operator was quite different from the native fleet. Ex-Somerbus of Paulton 3916 (K29 OEU) had 29-seat Wright Nimbus bodywork, on a 709D chassis. It is seen in Wells.

the bus by itself, with the diesel engine turned off. FirstBus was one of many transport organisations conducting practical trials of alternative forms of fuel or propulsion to help the environment.

While the changes were being made to the running units of No.100, the original shallow destination box was replaced by the later style of deeper box. The bus was then repainted into silver, with oversized FirstBus emblems, before being re-registered VCL 461. This 'cherished' numberplate was one of a set of 'dateless' marks obtained by Bristol O.C. in 1984 for a batch of acquired coaches that were past their first flush of youth, after which the mark was transferred to two other vehicles before ending up on Provincial's number 100.

In March 1997 there came another business acquisition, when Streamline Taxis of Bath was taken over by Bristol Omnibus Company. This brought in another ten Mercedes-Benz T2s. Nine had been bought new for services tendered by the then Avon County Council, while the tenth was a coach. Details of the Streamline fleet are given later. Streamline's operations were retained by the Bristol company as another separate division, though allied to the Badgerline division. By now, the Badgerline Mercs were being repainted from all-over bright green to the standard Badgerline yellow/bright green/yellow livery, as used on the full-sized buses, but now with the colour divisions sloping rearwards. A start was made at repainting the Streamline Mercs into a corresponding white/red/white style.

In October 1997, the 609D van-conversion acquired with the Durbin business three years earlier, E694 UND, was transferred to the Streamline fleet. Unexpectedly, it was re-numbered from 8945 and now re-used the number 3912, which had been vacant since the Beaver-609D had passed to Provincial, a year earlier. It was repainted in the white/red/white livery, but within a few months, it had been further repainted, into Badgerline's yellow/green/yellow. Despite that, it tended to continue

From 1997, Badgerline's Mercs were repainted into the standard livery as applied to 'big buses', now with the colour divisions sloping rearwards and with FirstBus style fleetnames. Another of the Weston-super-Mare 709Ds, 3854 (J854 FTC), shows off the style.

on the same services over restricted roads in the city of Bath.

In March 1999, Bristol Omnibus Company Ltd was renamed First Bristol Buses Ltd. Further renaming occurred in 2003, when, to absorb the now-related First Southern National Ltd, as outlined under that heading above, the Badgerline and Streamline divisions became parts of First Somerset & Avon Ltd – despite the County of Avon having been abolished as long ago as 1996.

Meanwhile, links within the FirstBus group were utilised in early 2001 when some contracted services run by Swift Link (Eurotaxis Ltd) of Harry Stoke, near Bristol, were cancelled by North Somerset Council. The Badgerline division was awarded the contracts instead, but extra midibuses were needed quickly. An interesting variety of ten K- to N-registered Mercedes-Benz 709Ds was obtained from former Badgerline Group member, and now a fellow FirstBus company, Potteries Motor Traction (PMT) of Stoke-on-Trent. Four carried the familiar Plaxton Beaver body, but another four carried Marshall C19 bodywork. The final two differed from any Badgerline Merc, as the bodywork here was the Dormobile Routemaker 2. The coachwork on these featured the round-cornered side windows.

Badgerline chose new numbers to match the last two digits of their registrations, so they were numbered 3934/41/2 (K434/41/2 XRF – Plaxton Beaver B24F), 3954-7 (L554, 455, 556/7 LVT – Marshall C19 B23F), 3974 (N574 CEH – Plaxton Beaver B22F) and 3994/5 (L494/5 HRE – Dormobile Routemaker 2 B24F). Eight were operated in PMT's yellow and red livery, while 3994/5 were in their 'Flexi' colours of white and blue, devised and originally branded for dedicated services. Circumstances allowed the buses to start their way back to the Potteries from the autumn of 2001, except that the Dormobile-bodied pair carried on further south, to First Western National.

Transfers were now being made to subsidiary fleets, with a repaint into a corporate style. An Optare StarRider that was moved to Durbin Coaches was 3817 (E817 MOU). It is awaiting students at the City Technical College in east Bristol.

Above: The yellow and red livery of Potteries Motor Traction offered an interesting contrast with the yellow and green livery of Badgerline on eight 709Ds drafted into the fleet early in 2001. Outside Weston-super-Mare Town Hall are seen 3934 (K434 XRF) with 3852 (J852 FTC).

Below: Marshall bodywork was carried by four of the PMT 709Ds, as shown by 3957 (L557 LVT), on the Bath circular 20A, at Parade Gardens. Note it still retains 'The Potteries Connection' wording on the cove panels.

Above: Now devoid of signwriting on its Flexi livery is one of two Mercs that brought the Dormobile Routemaker 2 bodywork into the Badgerline fleet. 3994 (L494 HRE) is standing at the terminus in Blagdon of service 673 from Bristol, the prime reason for obtaining these buses.

Below: Several Mercs were still an essential part of the First Somerset & Avon fleet in 2005, so they were treated to a repaint into First's prime 'Willowleaf' livery. The former 3904 (L904 VHT), now numbered 51104, was one of many that moved from Bath to Weston-super-Mare in later years, to release earlier examples. It stands outside the Winter Gardens on the sea-front.

The Wright Nimbus-bodied 811D looked impressive in Willowleaf livery. Formerly Southern National 757 (L651 CJT), it is now numbered 51211 and is just out of the paint-shop, so has yet to receive all identities. It is seen at work on a Weston-super-Mare town service, opposite the Town Hall.

The FirstBus 'Barbie 2' livery was adopted as standard for repaints in 2001 and this included a few of the PMT Mercs. The renumbering of the fleet into First's National system occurred in 2004, samples of which are given below. From April 2005, many of the surviving but still vital Mercedes-Benz midibuses were treated to a repaint into the prime FirstBus 'Willowleaf' livery, as had been applied to new buses since 1998, and this rejuvenated them.

Some unexpected extra activity came for the company's Mercs in 2009, as detailed below under the heading of ACL Travel.

BRISTOL OMNIBUS COMPANY LTD.

From early 1986, in advance of bus service deregulation, Bristol Omnibus Company started to place into service a fleet of seventy-five 16-seat Ford Transit minibuses on Bristol city services. They carried a livery of yellow, with red and blue bands, plus the fleet-name 'City Dart', the company itself now trading as City Line. Very soon afterwards, 25 Mercedes-Benz L608D 20-seaters joined the City Dart fleet and these were followed, on Deregulation Day itself (26 October 1986), by no fewer than seventy more L608Ds. A change was made in 1988 to the Iveco 49-10, with severe-looking Dormobile Routemaker bodywork. These looked bigger, but still contained 20 seats. From the end of 1988, while the forty-eight Ivecos were being placed in service, the sale of Ford Transits commenced.

City Line was bought from the NBC in 1987 in a joint bid between Bristol Omnibus Company's management and Midland Red West Holdings. Then, in 1988, the two companies accepted an offer made for them by the expanding Badgerline Group.

There followed a lull in proceedings until 1993. Rather late in the day it was decided that a new fleet of midibuses should start to replace the last few Transits and the first of the Merc L608Ds. The new buses were Mercedes-Benz 709Ds, with

THE MERCEDES-BENZ MIDIBUS IN SOUTH WEST ENGLAND • 125

Plaxton Beaver bodies. They contained only 22 seats, as thought had been given to providing luggage space. Although carrying a similar livery to the minibuses, the fleetname was the generic City Line.

The first batch comprised twenty-six buses, 7801-7826 (L801-826 SAE). The 1994 order called for a further forty-eight (7827-7874: L827-830 WHY, M831-874 ATC). The third and final order, for 1995, was affected, like Badgerline's later 709Ds, by certain registration numbers being withheld. So, the batch of thirty-one was numbered 7875-87/89-99 and 7901-7 (N875 HWS, etc. – note that Badgerline had similar Mercs with J-HWS marks).

In March 1995, City Line received for evaluation one of the first of the new Mercedes 711D models. It had been registered in May 1994 through Sheffield by the Mercedes-Benz headquarters in nearby Tankersley, as L707 LKY. It contained 23 seats, but was painted in full City Line midibus livery, with the fleetnumber 8707. Badgerline, at the same time, was also evaluating a 711D, with their own 3877 (L877 TFB), as recorded above.

Following the merger of the Badgerline Group with GRT Holdings in 1995 to form First Group, as mentioned above, Bristol Omnibus Company Ltd was renamed First Bristol Buses Ltd in March 1999, only for the Bristol city division to be separated again in August 2001, as First City Line Ltd. By now, the movement of Merc midibuses between the local constituents was familiar, several leaving City Line for First Southern National, in particular. The moves were usually followed by a repaint into the appropriate livery. From 2001, however, repainting adopted First's previously-described 'Barbie 2' livery.

In June 2003, another renaming occurred. On the occasion of the merger of First Southern National's Somerset area with First Bristol Buses Ltd, to form First Somerset & Avon Ltd, First City Line Ltd became – confusingly – First Bristol Ltd. Few Mercedes midibuses remained in service to receive the First Bristol Ltd legal-lettering. The following January, the First Bristol fleet was renumbered into First's national system, but only nine Mercs were still running in the city. Formerly 7803, etc., they now became 51003/025 (L803/825 SAE), 51029 (L829 WHY) and 51555/61/2/6-8 (M855 ATC, etc.).

Only a very small number of Mercs was ever transferred into the Bristol city fleet from First companies elsewhere in the country. One most unexpected and late arrival, though, was a 709D/Beaver from West Yorkshire. Of course, it carried a 'Nonsensical Northern Number', 50258. This, by pure chance, very nearly matched the registration number, of M259 VWU. It arrived in January 2005, by which time barely half-a-dozen native 709Ds were left in service. Remarkably, it outlived all of those.

Bristol Omnibus Company, trading as City Line since 1985, waited until 1993 before starting to replace its last minibuses with Mercedes-Benz 709D midibuses. Only 22 seats were installed, as there was a large luggage pen. A bus from the first batch, 7820 (L820 SAE), is seen turning off Broad Quay on a circular route that passed the zoo. Note Badgerline's emblem in the side window.

Above: Once City Line and Badgerline were under common management, the occasional transfer was made between them. Rarely, though, did a bus move *in* to the city fleet, but an exception was Badgerline's 3909 (L909 VHT), which is seen just after being repainted as a City Line bus, in July 1998. It is standing at the bus-station at the large Cribbs Causeway shopping centre.

Below: An even more unexpected occurrence was the transfer to the Bristol city fleet as late as January 2005, of a solitary 709D-Beaver from First West Yorkshire. The fleet-number allocated in the original, random, 2003 national renumbering scheme to M259 VWU managed to be just one out from the registration, by being 50258.

The arrival of 50258 was not the end of surprises. In January 2006, by which time the only Merc left in the Bristol city fleet was, remarkably, 50258, three Varios turned up. They spent most of their time on the 4 to the north-eastern suburbs, largely away from main roads. 52553 (S553 RWP) is seen here in Stapleton village.

A year later, an even more unexpected event was the addition of three Mercedes-Benz Varios. These were 52553/4/64 (S553/4/64 RWP), from the large batch new to Midland Red West.

CHELTENHAM & GLOUCESTER OMNIBUS COMPANY LTD

This company started preparing for Deregulation a year early, by placing in service a stock of thirty-five Ford Transit 16-seaters in October 1985. In the following spring, fourteen Mercedes-Benz L608D 20-seaters were added. A change to 25-seaters was made in the 1987/88 winter, through the choice of the MCW Metrorider, for another fourteen vehicles. In September 1988, though, C&GOC obtained, for assessment, a solitary Mercedes-Benz 709D. It carried a rare PMT Bursley body, seating 25, and was numbered in progression from the other small buses, as 677, being registered F677 PDF through Gloucester, as was normal for this company. It carried the company's Stroud Valleys livery, of mint-green, with a yellow flash. Directly afterwards, another 709D was taken for assessment, this being a demonstrator with Reeve Burgess Beaver B25F bodywork, F311 DET. This was purchased the following spring, as number 678.

The outcome of the trials was that, for a batch of six more 709Ds, it was PMT who was awarded the contract, for their Bursley body. This made it a very unusual batch. The six entered service in November 1989 as 679-684 (G679-684 AAD).

The company's small buses carried a distinctive livery of silver, with red and blue bands, upon

The Cheltenham & Gloucester Omnibus Company (C&GOC), after the trial of two assessment vehicles, ordered six Mercedes-Benz 709Ds with PMT Bursley bodywork – see Section 1. This was to become a rare combination. The company's silver Metro livery is shown by 682 (G682 AAD), in Clarence Street, Gloucester, on a city service.

which was carried the fleetname Metro. There were, though, a few exceptions and, besides 677, Beaver-bodied 678 was painted in the 'Cotswold' livery otherwise reserved for coaches. This was white, with bands in mint-green and truck-red, both shades being featured on the 'big buses' in the C&GOC fleet. Furthermore, PMT-bodied 679 was delivered in Cotswold livery (but with a leaf-green band in error, rather than mint-green).

Only a month after entering service, 681 was involved in a serious accident. It was delicenced while it was extensively rebuilt and did not re-enter service until March 1991.

No more new Mercs arrived until 1993. In the January, the Swindon & District division received just two examples, these being 33-seat 811Ds, carrying Wright Nimbus bodywork, in this division's own truck-red and cream livery. They started a new numbering series for larger small buses, as 801/2, and were registered through Swindon as K801/2 OMW. In the September there came another four 811D 33-seaters, but these looked very different, as 803-6 (L803-6 XDG) carried altogether squarer Marshall C16 bodies and were painted in green and yellow Stroud Valleys livery.

It should be pointed out that by now, the C&GOC 'Group' consisted of three operations, Cheltenham & Gloucester Omnibus Co Ltd, Cheltenham District Traction Co Ltd (formed on 1 August 1993) and Swindon & District Bus Co Ltd (formed on 1 December 1991). There was also a substantial interest in Circle Line of Gloucester, but this retained its own identity as a low-cost

Above: In 1993, the semi-autonomous Swindon & District Bus Company was allocated two Mercedes-Benz 811Ds, with Wright Nimbus 33-seat bodies. These were evidently regarded as 'big buses' and carried that division's truck-red and cream livery, rather than the Metro silver that was carried by their MCW Metroriders. 801 (K801 OMW) is en route for Marlborough and Savernake Hospital.

Below: Later in 1993, C&GOC's Stroud Valleys division received four 811D 33-seaters, but bodied by Marshall, to their altogether squarer style. 805 (L805 XDG) reverses off the platform at Gloucester bus-station, bound for its home town. Leonard Stanley is *not* the name of the driver.

unit. Transfers between each subsidiary occurred when necessary.

To facilitate its purchase from the NBC, which had happened as early as the end of October 1986, C&GOC had set up a holding company, named Western Travel. Subsequently, the Western Travel organisation was used to purchase the whole or part of two of C&GOC's neighbouring NBC operators. Midland Red South was purchased in December 1987, then, in December 1990, Western Travel assumed responsibility for the eastern area of National Welsh Omnibus Services, for which the Red & White name was revived. It is interesting to note that, in 1989, Midland Red South took delivery of three PMT Bursley-bodied 709Ds at the same time that C&GOC received their 679-684 and that Red & White received a pair of similar buses in August 1991.

Western Travel was then sold, in December 1993, to the Stagecoach group, whose origins are explained above, under the Devon General heading. The Gloucestershire and Wiltshire operations were to be known as Stagecoach West. A major outcome of the take-over was that, from the summer of 1994, the C&GOC fleets started to be refreshed with fifty new Stagecoach-standard Mercedes-Benz 709Ds, with Alexander Sprint B25F bodies, in the white livery with 'toothpaste' stripes. They were numbered from 685 to 735, excluding 700, and were registered through Gloucester, except for the seven for Swindon & District (711-7), which were dealt with locally – i.e., L685-696 CDD, M697-9/701-3 EDD, M704-710 JDG, then M711-5 FMR and N716/7 KAM and, finally, N718-735 RDD. No further Mercs were received new, as the companies turned to lightweight, then low-floor single-deckers.

A small number of Mercs was transferred in, however, from other Stagecoach fleets, inasmuch as other examples were moved out. The preferred model was the 811D, so these took the numbers 807 upwards. Not surprisingly, transfers from

In December 1993, C&GOC's parent, the Western Travel Group, was sold to Stagecoach. Quickly, no fewer than fifty 'Stagecoach-standard' Alexander Sprint 25-seat Mercedes-Benz 709Ds were allocated to C&GOC and Swindon & District. One of the later ones, 735 (N735 RDD) is seen at Stroud's Subscription Rooms, on a local service. The strapline beneath the Stagecoach fleetname still states Stroud Valleys.

Above: Repainting the fleet into Stagecoach white soon got under way, with some novel results. Here, for example, is PMT Bursley-bodied 683 (G683 AAD). It is in Cirencester, which, surprisingly, had its own name on the strapline.

Below: Stagecoach livery, as it looked on a Wright Nimbus 811D. Swindon & District's 802 (K802 OMW) is seen in 1995. The following year, however, both 801/2 were transferred to Circle Line of Gloucester and fitted with wheelchair lifts at the back, for operation on disabled persons' transport.

A Marshall-811D in Stagecoach stripes. Stroud Valleys 803 (L803 XDG) is another to be seen at the town's Subscription Rooms.

Red & White or Midland Red South were more prevalent, these J- and K-registered examples carrying Wright Nimbus bodies. Meanwhile, as early as 1996, similar native buses 801/2 (K801/2 OMW) were transferred from Swindon & District to Circle Line of Gloucester, where they were fitted with tail lifts and adapted to carry passengers in wheelchairs. Their Stagecoach stripes were overpainted with a single, broad, green band. PMT Bursley-bodied 680-2 followed them and received the same broad, green band, as did some ex-Midland Red South Mercs. In January 2000, however, Circle Line was closed down and their buses were absorbed by C&GOC.

As late as 2002, seven more Mercs were transferred from Red & White. These were long tailed 711Ds which, it was decided, should be numbered in the 800s. 820-2 were P167/71 TNY and P161 TDW and these had Plaxton Beaver bodies, an unusual shape for the C&GOC fleets. Even more unusual were 817/8/23/4 (N152/3/8/9 MTG), as these carried uncommon WS or UVG Wessex II bodywork. They had all started life with Rhondda Buses, which was another successor to National Welsh, and which went on to be taken over by Stagecoach in 1997.

The national renumbering of all the Stagecoach fleets into a single series took place in January 2003. The lowest number applied to a Merc in this fleet was 40644, which went to N644 VSS, the last survivor of three ex-Stagecoach Cambus/Viscount 709D-Sprints that had been intended for Stagecoach Bluebird Buses of Aberdeen. This one was latterly numbered 736. Native examples that were still in the fleet, 718 onwards (N718 RDD, etc), became 40718, etc. The 711Ds and the 811Ds were placed in the 41000s, with the seven ex-Red & White buses being numbered

Above: Transferred from Red & White in 2002 were seven late model 711Ds, with long tailed 27-seat bodies. 821 (P171 TNY) and two sisters carried Plaxton Beaver coachwork, a design only seen previously in the C&GOC fleet on the assessment bus, 678 (F311 DET). 821 is shown in Clarence Street, Gloucester, soon after its arrival. *Dave Russell & Deric Pemberton.*

Below: Even rarer types added to the fleet were four 711Ds with long tailed WS or UVG Wessex II bodies. Seen here is 818 (N153 MTG). All seven commenced life with Rhondda Buses, which was acquired by Stagecoach in 1997. Some went on to serve Faresaver of Chippenham, which is detailed below. *Dave Russell & Deric Pemberton.*

between 41152 and 41171, and the others up to 41806 (L806 XDG), all in accordance with their registration numbers.

In the summer of 2005, yet more Alexander Sprint 709Ds were transferred from Red & White, but no renumbering was required this time, of course.

In March 2006, a small operator in the Forest of Dean, to the west of the River Severn, suddenly ceased trading. Stagecoach West took on the services and the varied fleet, but soon, as non-standard stock was put aside, three Mercedes-Benz midibuses were transferred in to Coleford, from Stagecoach Thames Transit. Interestingly, the three arrivals were Varios, a type not previously encountered in the West fleet. They were 42376 (S376 DFC), which carried an Alexander ALX100 body, and 42586/8 (T586/8 SKG), which had Plaxton Beaver 2 bodies and which had been new to Phil Anslow of Garndiffaith, near

Drafted in to cover the demise of a small operator in the Forest of Dean were three Mercedes-Benz Varios. Coming from Stagecoach Thames Transit was 42376 (S376 DFC), which carried Alexander ALX100 bodywork. It displays the post-2001 Stagecoach livery as it swings into Lydney bus-station, soon after arriving with the West company. *Dave Russell & Deric Pemberton.*

Standing at Coleford Market Place is one of the two Plaxton Beaver 2-bodied Varios drafted into the Forest of Dean, 42586 (T586 SKG). It originally ran for Phil Anslow of Garndiffaith, Pontypool. *Dave Russell & Deric Pemberton.*

Pontypool. Very soon, another former Anslow bus joined them, this time a 709D with WS Wessex II bodywork, M92 JHB (40595). Ex-Red & White 711Ds 41152/159/171 were also moved to Coleford.

THAMESDOWN TRANSPORT LTD.
Besides Plymouth Citybus Ltd, the only other municipally owned bus company in this region was Thamesdown Transport Ltd of Swindon, in north Wiltshire. Their choice for their small midibus fleet, however, was the Dodge 50-series. Most were bodied by Northern Counties, who had been the Swindon concern's favoured bodybuilder in the 1960s and again in the 1980s.

WILTS & DORSET BUS COMPANY LTD.
Wilts & Dorset avoided taking any 16-seat minibuses into its fleet and waited until 1987 before taking any small buses at all. In its choice, though, Wilts & Dorset was unusual, in standardising on the MCW Metrorider. It quickly built up a large fleet and followed these up with further examples after Optare had taken over the design and reworked it. They also bought a number of low-mileage MCW versions second-hand.

Wilts & Dorset never operated a Mercedes-Benz in their own fleet, but the acquisition of some small operators brought a few examples into common ownership.

SMALL OPERATORS

At the end of the twentieth century and the start of the twenty-first, there was a vast number of small operators in the south-west, many of which owned at least a few Mercedes-Benz T2 van-conversions or midibuses. There were some fleets, though, in which the T2 played a significant role. Many small businesses made a meagre living on services that were financially supported by the local councils, through contracts won by tendering – and often lost just as quickly. In other instances, operators were putting up a sphere of competition against an incumbent operator and T2s were an inexpensive yet very efficient way to keep their operating costs down.

In most cases, the variant of T2 chosen by the small operators was dependent on what was available on the second-hand market at the time the buses were needed. The first owners, it should be noted, were not selling off T2s through any dislike or dissatisfaction, but principally due to changing market needs, or from losing contracts themselves. Often, the T2 was a victim of its own success – it had generated more passenger traffic, so a larger bus needed to be substituted. The requirement to progress to fully-accessible low-floor buses also had a bearing on the life-span of T2s with first owners.

STREAMLINE BUSES (BATH) LTD.
Following bus service deregulation in October 1986, Streamline won some of the first contracts for supported services issued by Avon County Council. These were mainly evening and Sunday duties in and around Bath, on what, at other times, would be Badgerline routes. A selection of small buses was used, from Ford, Freight Rover and Iveco.

In March 1988, Streamline added a new Mercedes Benz midi-coach to their fleet. The chassis was a 609D, but, as was quite common in that era, it carried coach-built Reeve-Burgess Beaver bodywork, with 25 coach seats. It was registered E339 MHU and was one of the first of the breed in the south-west, arriving even before Badgerline or Devon General had received their first T2s. It remained with Streamline until September 1992, when it passed locally to Berkeley Coaches of Paulton, who continued to run it for another 14 years.

It was in 1992 that Streamline won the contract for a pair of services on the east side of Bristol, the 532/533, from Downend, via Hanham, to Keynsham. For these services, Streamline placed in service, in January 1993, five new Mercedes-Benz 709Ds, with Plaxton Beaver B23F bodies, K690-694 UFV. Their Preston registrations showed

A very early T2 was E339 MHU with Streamline of Bath. It carried a Reeve-Burgess Beaver coach-type body, yet with a folding door. Indeed, it is seen here working on the Avon County Council supported Bath city circular service, later renumbered 20A/20C.

that, in the same way as two of those with Clapton Coaches, mentioned under the Badgerline heading, these were supplied by Ciceley Commercials of Blackburn. The attractive livery was white, with red skirt and roof, plus red and black fleetnames.

Further contract wins saw the arrival in September 1994 of four new 811Ds, with Marshall B31F bodies, also in the white and red. This time they were registered by the body-builder, as M45-48 BEG.

Streamline followed these buses by one more coach-specification T2. In contrast to E339 MHU, the 25-seat 609D-Beaver, M968 USC was a 33-seat 814D-Beaver. Again, it carried the company's coach livery of white, with staggered red stripes.

Streamline later started competing against First Badgerline on the service from Bath city centre to the University, using new DAF/Ikarus single-deckers. After more than a year of rivalry, the situation was resolved in March 1997, by Bristol Omnibus Company acquiring Streamline. The Bristol company decided to keep Streamline as a low-cost subsidiary, so the fleet remained intact. The stock was given fleetnumbers, however. As so often, although the batches were kept together, the numbers were allocated to each batch in reverse order of age. The 709Ds became 8311-5 (K690-4 UFV), the 811Ds became 8307-10 (M45-48 BEG) and the 814D coach became 8306 (M968 USC).

In a very strange move, Bristol Omnibus Company accepted an offer to sell the registration number of 8309 – M47 BEG – to a private owner, for use on a car. This happened early in 1999. The Merc had to be re-registered, of course, the new Bristol mark issued being M857 XHY.

Before long, the Streamline livery was changed to use the Badgerline style of diagonally divided colours, in the form of white/red/white, with FirstBus-style Streamline names. Streamline individuality was lost, though, once the FirstBus 'Barbie 2' livery was introduced in 2001 and further anonymity followed with the renumbering into First's National scheme in 2004.

Above: Streamline of Bath won the contract for a pair of services on the east side of Bristol, from January 1993. To work the 532/533, five new 709Ds, with Plaxton Beaver 23-seat bodies, were purchased. K690 UFV is resting at the Downend shops, having arrived from Keynsham, via Hanham.

Below: Further contract wins in 1994 were met with the arrival of four new 811Ds, with 31-seat Marshall bodies. M46 BEG is seen in 1998 leaving the University of the West of England (UWE), located on the northern outskirts of Bristol, on another contracted service.

Above: Another Mercedes coach with a Beaver body arrived in 1994, but M968 USC was a 33-seater, on 814D chassis. It is seen standing adjacent to the Bath bus station. *Bristol Vintage Bus Group.*

Below: After Streamline became a subsidiary of First Bristol, extra Mercs started to be transferred to the fleet and repainted in a new Streamline livery, in Badgerline house style. Here, Optare StarRider 3821 (E821 MOU) is seen at Parade Gardens on a Bath city service.

Above: The newest of the Mercs acquired by First Bristol with the Clapton Coaches business, 3915 (L390 UHU), was later transferred from Badgerline to Streamline, with a repaint, as can be seen here.

Below: K694 UFV passes E694 UND, outside Bath bus station. Things were getting complex now – 709D-Beaver K694 UFV was ex-Streamline 8315, but was now in Badgerline livery, while 609D van-conversion E694 UND, formerly Durbin Coaches 8945, was now in Streamline livery, as the second 3912, numbered amid the ex-Clapton Mercs.

Above: Just another FirstBus Beaver-bodied Merc? Not quite. J850 OBV started life with Clapton Coaches, then was taken over by Badgerline, transferred later to Streamline, and is now in its fourth livery, the FirstBus 'Barbie 2' scheme. The MH prefix to its number 3914 stems from a short term allocation to Marlborough Street in Bristol, but it should have reverted to BH, for Bath, by now.

Below: First's Willowleaf livery was given to the ex-Streamline Marshall-bodied 811Ds, as shown by 51346 (M46 BEG). It is seen at the exit of a temporary Bath bus-station, used while extensive redevelopment was taking place around the old site.

EUROTAXIS AND SWIFT LINK, HARRY STOKE, SOUTH GLOS.

Mr Juan Sanzo began operations as Northavon Taxis before registering the name Eurotaxis in 1991. Acquired that year were two Mercedes-Benz 609D/Reeve Burgess van conversions. In 1994, a major expansion of work occurred by the winning of an Avon County Council tender for the services southwards from Bristol to the Chew Valley. This was met by Eurotaxis buying four new Mercedes-Benz 811D 33-seaters. The buses received the first production coach-built bodies to full PSV standards to be designed for the T2 by Mellor, as described in Section 1, under that maker's heading. The four were fitted with coach seats and had seat belts, together with front, rear and side destination boxes. Eurotaxis' minibuses had carried a plain white livery, but for these new midibuses, Eurotaxis specified that they should be red, with yellow bonnets.

They introduced a new fleetname, of Swift Link, incorporating the outline of a swift in flight.

They were supplied through a dealer in Leicestershire (Cossington Commercials), who had them registered through Leicester VLO, as M45-48 GRY; it will be noticed that at the same time, and by remarkable coincidence, Streamline of Bath received four Marshall-bodied 811Ds with registrations M45-48 BEG.

Eurotaxis was keen to expand and, with Mellor producing two 709Ds with long tailed B27F bodies for stock, Eurotaxis bought the pair (registered by Mellor through Manchester as M675/6 TNA). These retained their white paintwork, but with blue Swift Link names. Before long, they were both repainted into the red and yellow Swift Link livery.

Early in 1996, Eurotaxis bought four former London Transport Optare StarRiders, the former SR17, 18, 97 & 102 (F917/8 YWY and

Bought by Eurotaxis for Avon County Council-funded services south from Bristol to the Chew Valley, bounded by Somerset's Mendip Hills, were four new Mercedes-Benz 811Ds, painted in their new Swift Link livery. They carried the first purpose-built PSV bodies for the T2 chassis to be built by Mellor. M45 GRY waits to enter Bristol bus-station, in Marlborough Street.

Also on the 673 is one of two 709D 27-seaters bought from Mellor stock, M675 TNA. White paintwork with blue lettering was customary in the existing Eurotaxis fleet. It is seen at the other end of Bristol's bus-station.

G97, 102 KUB). Of course, with their wide doorways and standing space, there were only 26 seats. Nevertheless, they were put to work on a Bristol city service to the University of the West of England (UWE) at Frenchay. The service competed with Bristol City Line, although the StarRiders supported a batch of acquired Bristol VR double-deckers. A further StarRider was former Bebb of Llantwit Fardre H82 PTG, this running in a silver-blue colour.

At the end of that year, Eurotaxis won the hastily re-issued contract for Bristol city routes 585-587, following the previous holder's contracts being cancelled. These routes were handled mainly with a consignment of used Iveco 49-10s, but the routes did expand the sphere of operation for the Merc T2s on occasion. At the contract's full term, only six months later, Eurotaxis was outbid by Bristol City Line, which illustrates the precarious nature of dependence on contracted work.

Eurotaxis by now, though, was greatly expanding the provision of school transport, including for special schools, and started to amass a huge fleet of minibuses. Their choice was largely the T1 series of Mercedes-Benz, ranging from the 208D to the 410D, and, in later years, the choice was the Sprinter, up to 616CDi trim – twice the power for the same weight as an L608D. Most of the T2s that came were van conversions, as well. The company also developed a coaching unit.

As stated under the Badgerline heading, in 2001 North Somerset Council felt obliged to cancel the contract Eurotaxis held for the Chew Valley routes. The four Mellor-bodied 811Ds remained, however, as useful members

THE MERCEDES-BENZ MIDIBUS IN SOUTH WEST ENGLAND • 143

Above: Eurotaxis started working commercial services out to the aforementioned UWE in 1996. Four former London SR-class Optare StarRiders joined the Swift Link fleet, such as G97 KUB, seen on the 80A approaching the UWE.

Below: Mellor-bodied 709D M675 TNA is seen again, but after being repainted into the Swift Link red, although with simplified fleet-names. This time it is depicted working through Westbury-on-Trym, in north-west Bristol, on the 585, one of the set of contracted and somewhat round-about city services, gained from City Line in 1996.

of the fleet. In fact, a fifth example joined them that year – N627 BWG. This retained all-white paintwork (it is shown in Section 1). In early 2006, three of the original Mellor-811Ds, M45-47 GRY, passed together to Group Travel of Bodmin, Cornwall.

Although the contracts for the 585-587 had been lost in 1997, Eurotaxis successfully retendered for the slightly revised versions in 2006, which resulted in an influx of rather different Mercs. As it happened, the Glasgow dealer Blythswood Motors had taken back into stock several Mercs that had been supplied new by them (so registered through Glasgow) to small operators around Motherwell and Paisley and these formed the bulk of a stock of ten Mercs that Eurotaxis obtained for the 584-587. The novel aspect of these was that they were all Mercedes-Benz Varios, a type rarely found in this region. Furthermore, bodywork by Plaxton only appeared on four of the ten, which went against the general trend. Another four had much less common coachwork, in the form of the Marshall Master. The final two Varios happened to have been bodied by a firm that was well represented in Eurotaxis' original Swift Link fleet, namely Mellor. By now, however, only one of the Mellor T2s remained in the fleet – N627 BWG.

Eurotaxis had discontinued its Swift Link identity, so all ten Varios ran in the white livery in which they were acquired. The Mellor-bodied Varios were S612 HGD and S280 LGA. Those with Marshall Master bodies were S281 LGA, S370 PGB, S578 RGA and T578 KGB. The Plaxton Beaver 2 was only carried by R955 FYS, S751 LGA and a rather newer bus, still carrying the name of Speedwell of Glossop, MX04 VMJ. The fourth Plaxton-Vario was an odd one out – R620 GFS carried the original style of Beaver body, because this was in coach form. As such, with no destination box and nowhere to mount a ticket machine or cash tray, it was, of course, rather unsuitable for stage-carriage work in a city.

Remarkably, Mellor coachwork re-appeared in the Eurotaxis fleet in 2006, but this time on Mercedes-Benz Vario chassis. Short-wheelbase S612 HGD had started life on Clydeside but is shown here passing through Clifton in Bristol. All Eurotaxis Varios remained in the white paintwork in which they were acquired.

Above: Four of the Eurotaxis Varios carried uncommon Marshall Master bodywork. The distinctive style is shown by S281 LGA, which is leaving Westbury-on-Trym village in Bristol. This bus is another short wheelbase model.

Below: The offside aspect of the Marshall Master bodywork, here on long wheelbase T578 KGB. Once again, the bus is in Westbury-on-Trym, this time heading across the northern suburbs to Kingswood.

Eurotaxis' Swift Link colours were recalled by the operation of an Autobus Nouvelle 2 in the red it carried on acquisition from Martin Perry's Bromyard Omnibus Company. X346 AVJ is seen in Clifton again.

At the same time, Eurotaxis won some evening and Sunday contracts on what, during the daytime, were services worked by Bristol City Line or by South Gloucestershire Bus & Coach. These contracts also employed the Varios, as again shown in Section 1.

Unfortunately, Eurotaxis found that the 584-587 did not live up to expectations and they surrendered all these contracts early the next year. Some of the Varios quickly returned to Blythswood Motors. Marshall Master-bodied S281 LGA, however, passed to Carmel Coaches in Devon, only to return to the Bristol area in 2011, to operate on tendered services in Bath, and even into Bristol. It was now run by Young (CT Coaches) of Radstock. Another bus to go south-west was ex-Speedwell MX04 VMJ, as this was acquired by Western Greyhound of Summercourt, Cornwall, a business described below. Western Greyhound later re-registered this bus locally – as was their wont – to WK04 KUO.

SOUTH GLOUCESTERSHIRE BUS & COACH AND WESSEXCONNECT.

The driving force behind South Gloucestershire Bus & Coach was Roger Durbin, who had been in business for many years, in the footsteps of his father, Arthur. In 1994, Roger's business was acquired by the Badgerline Group and placed under Bristol Omnibus Company management. After the requisite number of years absent from operations, as part of the conditions of sale, Roger Durbin returned to business and set up South Gloucestershire Bus & Coach in 1998, from his old premises at Patchway Station. An eye-catching kingfisher-blue and white livery was adopted.

Initially following schools and coaching activities once again, in 2000 South Gloucestershire started submitting successful tenders for local service bus work, from Bristol City Council and South Gloucestershire Council. A variety of single-deckers was bought for this work, but before long, a selection of

THE MERCEDES-BENZ MIDIBUS IN SOUTH WEST ENGLAND • 147

Mercedes-Benz T2 midibuses started to appear on the routes. Some variety came with these, as exemplified by some of the first acquisitions, both coming from Tillingbourne of Cranleigh – H422 GPM, a 709D with Phoenix bodywork, and J430 PPF, a 709D carrying Dormobile Routemaker 2 bodywork.

G900 TJA was an 811D of particular interest. This bus had bodywork by Mellor and it is believed to have been the first full-sized midibus body to have been built by the Rochdale firm. As explained under the Mellor heading in Section 1 of this book, the career of G900 TJA started in 1990 in Gloucestershire, by coincidence, but with the County Council, as a welfare bus, with a tail-lift for wheelchairs. It was sold after only two years. A subsequent owner, Rover Bus Service of Chesham, Bucks, converted the body to a 32-seater, with coach seats it is believed. It retained the door in the centre of the otherwise unglazed rear wall. Interestingly, it next passed to Stevensons of Uttoxeter and, hence, to Midland Red North, where it possessed bus seats. Only later were windows added either side of the door in the back, to produce a layout that was possibly unique on a coachbuilt Merc. With South Gloucestershire, it carried a 'reversed' livery of white, with Kingfisher-blue relief, as shown in Section 1.

Before long, several of the ubiquitous Beaver-bodied Mercs appeared in the fleet, on both 709D and 811D chassis, seating anything from 23 to 33. Of interest was the fact that three 811Ds new to Yorkshire Woollen District (L776/8/9 RWW) featured wide, London-style, 'double-width' doorways, which limited the seating to a maximum of 31. The three lengths of bus were mixed in service. After just a few years, the purchasing policy moved over to full-sized buses.

In 2007, in an unusual move, South Gloucestershire was approached by Flights-Hallmark of Birmingham, a large company with extensive operations across the country.

South Gloucestershire Bus & Coach won service work in 2000 with contracts from both Bristol and South Gloucestershire Councils. Some novel Mercedes-Benz T2s were soon obtained. Formerly with Tillingbourne of Cranleigh, Surrey, H422 GPM carried Phoenix 27-seat bodywork, to the Robin Hood design. It is passing through Westbury-on-Trym on its way into Bristol from Severn Beach.

Above: Travelling the opposite way, out of Westbury village, is J430 PPF, a 29-seater with handsome Dormobile Routemaker 2 coachwork. This also began life with Tillingbourne of Cranleigh.

Below: The Reeve-Burgess or Plaxton Beaver-bodied Merc soon formed the standard intake, as this 2002 view shows. J297 NNB, a 27-seat 709D, was new to Arrowline of Knutsford, but came from Arriva Cymru, while L779 RWW, a 31-seat 811D, was one of three new to Yorkshire Woollen District, although later with Arriva on Merseyside. They are working on services across Bristol's northern suburbs.

Above: H204 EKO had been the only Carlyle-bodied 709D in Maidstone & District's small midibus fleet. It later ran with Faresaver of Chippenham, then with Juliet's of Bristol on Portishead locals, before joining SGB&C at the age of 14 years. It is seen 6th April 2006 in Zetland Road, Redland, on the last weekday that the 586 reached this area of Bristol, this being abandoned with the re-awarding of the contract to Eurotaxis.

Below: When Wessexconnect took over the remaining contracted services from SGB&C in late 2007, they obtained their own Mercs. All were Varios, but among them were three with Alexander ALX100 bodies, including T471 HNH. It is seen at Bristol Parkway Station, on the 518.

They were interested in taking over all the Council contracted work from SGB&C. Roger Durbin accepted the offer. The process started piecemeal, not being completed until March 2008. Flights-Hallmark had set up Wessexconnect to run the local services, but few of the South Gloucestershire buses were transferred. Instead, Wessexconnect tended to acquire their own buses, or transfer them from Centralconnect in the Midlands, or from Surreyconnect. Only a few Mercedes-Benz midibuses were obtained for the Wessexconnect fleet, but all were Varios. Although most of these carried Plaxton Beaver 2 bodies, three interesting examples were T454, 456 & 471 HNH, as these carried Alexander ALX100 bodywork.

In May 2009, Wessexconnect won the contract to run Bath city's circular services 20A/20C. Accordingly, ALX100s T454/6 HNH were repainted black, with suitable signwriting. They were joined by Beaver 2-bodied V394 SVV.

Wessexconnect later started to build up a considerable fleet of low-floor Dennis-Plaxton 'Mini Pointer Darts' and the Mercedes fleet was subsequently eliminated. Certainly, none remained to receive the subsequent Wessex Red livery. Wessex underwent mixed fortunes, losing several contracts at re-tendering, but gaining some others. They also had spells of competing with First in Bristol, but eventually decided to withdraw from the region, passing operations, though very few buses, to Stagecoach West (Cheltenham & Gloucester Omnibus Company), in September 2018.

FARESAVER, CHIPPENHAM, WILTSHIRE

Originally running as Fosseway Faresaver, named after the Roman road that runs south-west through Wiltshire, the company run by the Pickford family used to use the tagline 'Go On All-fours', referring to their telephone number of Chippenham 444444. The company even obtained the special and highly suitable number-plate PSV 444. This has been carried by a range of vehicles over time.

A lot of work began after Deregulation in 1986 and many of Fosseway Faresaver's second-hand Ford Transits could be seen over a wide area

Faresaver of Chippenham began their love affair with the Mercedes-Benz T2 midibus in 1997, when two new 33-seat Marshall-bodied 814Ds were obtained. They were some of the last T2s to be built. P325 TGS is shown on a competing Bath city route, via Twerton to Whiteway.

of the county and as far away as Bristol. Around 1996, Faresaver took the chance to replace many Transits with a number of ex-Plymouth Citybus Dodge S56s, with Reeve-Burgess B23F bodywork. Meanwhile, in 1993 a solitary Optare StarRider 33-seater had been acquired. It was three-year-old G840 LWR. This was the company's introduction to the coachbuilt T2. A second, though coach-seated, StarRider, F430 AYG, followed in 1996 (together with yet more Transits), and also coming was L698 AGA, a Wadham Stringer B33F-bodied 811D, from Shuttle Buses of Kilwinning.

History was made in March 1997, however, when Faresaver placed in service two brand new 33-seat Merc T2s. The buses, P324/5 TGS, being late model T2s, were to the more-powerful 814D specification. They carried Marshall C16 bodywork. They were some of the last T2s to be built.

These two 814Ds may not have had a long life in Faresaver's hands (three years), but the seed was sown and from 1999, used T2s of all shapes and sizes began joining the fleet. This is exemplified by some of the earliest acquisitions – F328 FCY, a former South Wales Transport 814D/Robin Hood B31F; F125/8 TRU, one time Metrobus of Orpington 709Ds with Reeve-Burgess Beaver B25F; F70 RPL and G301 CPL, more Optare StarRiders, coming direct from Metrobus; H882 LOX, an 811D, with wide-doorway Carlyle C17 B28F, originally London's MC2, though by way of Stagecoach Fife Scottish; H204 EKO, a 709D/Carlyle from Arriva Kent & Sussex; and H523 SWE and H641 UWE, a 709D and an 811D respectively, with rare Whittaker-Europa Enterprise bodywork and mentioned under the Whittaker heading in Section 1; these were latterly with Arriva The Shires.

Before long, Faresaver began covering commercial services run by Badgerline, even within the city of Bath. Faresaver therefore bought a great number of second-hand Mercs, a lot coming from Arriva fleets, several initially running in Arriva livery. There was no Arriva operation in this area, though, so there was no clash of identity.

These acquisitions brought other types of bodywork into the fleet, such as the Alexander Sprint, the Dormobile Routemaker 2 and the Wright Nimbus, as well as more Carlyle/

Early-style Reeve-Burgess Beaver bodywork was carried by two 709Ds new to Metrobus of Orpington. F125 TRU, also on the 5, shows the yellow, white and blue variation of the livery.

Above: More livery variations, as well as coachwork variations, are shown on these two Mercs. The nearer bus, F328 FCY, is an ex-South Wales 814D with Robin Hood body, while passing it is the then latest PSV 444 – an Optare StarRider that was formerly G301 CPL with Metrobus.

Below: Over fifty short wheelbase 811Ds, with Carlyle 29-seat bodies, were supplied to the Transit Holdings fleets. Several later came to Faresaver, including the first such bus, H985 FTT. It is seen ready for the 231, Bath to Chippenham route, while standing ahead of a Bath Bus Company Dennis Dart.

Above: Faresaver chose new colours of white and mauve in 2002. 811D K138 BRF, new to Stevensons of Spath, has the variation of the Dormobile Routemaker 2 coachwork in which the side windows have rounded corners.

Below: Similar-aged 811D K365 TJF has the alternative Dormobile Routemaker 2 styling, in which the side windows have square corners. This one was new to Shamrock (Jones) of Pontypridd.

Above: One of the first used Mercs to be bought by Faresaver was deemed worthy of a repaint into the new colours. Thirteen-year-old H523 SWE, a 709D carrying one of the first bus-seated bodies to be built by Whittaker's Europa Coaches, was mentioned under that heading in Section 1. Sister bus H641 UWE, illustrated in the Whittaker section, was not only repainted in this livery, but also re-registered with the prestigious number PSV 444.

Above: Offering a comparison with Whittaker-bodied H523 SWE is N603 JGP, another 709D, but on this, the Whittaker-designed bodywork was constructed by Crystals of Doncaster. It was one of a batch built for Crystals' own bus operation, around Dartford in Kent. One major change in construction is a relocation of the main body pillars.

Above: Arriva fleets were a useful source for Mercs, and many were placed in service by Faresaver in Arriva's distinctive livery. L318 AUT, a 709D with Alexander (Belfast) Sprint bodywork, was new to Midland Fox, latterly Arriva Fox County. It is competing on First's 14 to the Royal United Hospital in Bath.

Below: Faresaver took the chance to acquire several late 811Ds that had been built with WS or UVG Wessex II bodies, for operators in the greater Glasgow region. These included N253 PGD.

Marshall and Reeve-Burgess/Plaxton products. Furthermore, the bodies on a number of late-model T2s supplied new to fleets on Clydeside were of the Wessex II design by WS or UVG. Indeed, only three of the twelve bodybuilders covered in Section 1 of this book were never featured in the Faresaver service bus fleet. They were Mellor, PMT and Ireland's Euro Coach.

Things came round full circle in 2006, when Faresaver acquired three P-registered Marshall C16-bodied T2s, even if this time P230/5/7 EJW were 811Ds with 31-seats.

With so many second-hand T2s available, Faresaver seemed not to be in the slightest bit interested in the Mercedes-Benz Vario. If they wanted to continue their following for Mercs, though, that had to change. It was, however, August 2006 before they placed in service their first Vario. This was S101 KNR, an O814. It had very uncommon bodywork, by Leicester Carriage Builders – almost as if it was deliberately chosen to add to the variety. The following March, this bus became the latest to bear the registration PSV 444.

The next month saw three more Varios arrive, this time carrying Alexander ALX100 bodies, but to the original, short lived pattern. They were very early Varios, being registered P112/3/7 HCH and had been part of a fleet of twenty-five new to Midland Fox nine years earlier. Subsequently, a large number of Varios entered the fleet, though almost all of these were less distinctive, in carrying Plaxton Beaver 2 bodywork.

Remarkably, in 2007, the Faresaver fleet comprised around sixty Mercedes-Benz T2 and Vario midibuses and just one Dennis Dart. Subsequently, though, more and more medium and large single-deckers were obtained – and even double-deckers in time – and the stock of Mercs was gradually eliminated.

Faresaver had a fondness for re-registering their buses with 'dateless' numbers, very many being of Northern Irish origin. The livery applied to its buses changed as time went on. Initially, buses were white and blue, then yellow was added before being simplified to yellow and blue. It has to be said this had a resemblance to the yellow and green of Badgerline, whose buses Faresaver often rivalled, not only in Wiltshire but on Bath city routes as well. After FirstBus adopted their 'Barbie 2' off-white and blue, with magenta

It was August 2006 before Faresaver bought their first Mercedes-Benz Vario. The initial example was S101 KNR, with rare Leicester Carriage Builders bodywork. It was soon given the honour of carrying the registration PSV 444, as seen in this view at Bath's Parade Gardens.

Further Varios followed, but as if determined to be different, early arrivals had the Mark I version of the Alexander ALX100 body. They included P117 HCH, which had been new to Midland Fox.

'fades', Faresaver turned to white and lilac – again, there was a resemblance.

The Pickford family was involved in dealing and hiring out, using the NextBus trading name, so if a good offer was received for a bus in the existing fleet, it could be sold, to be replaced by something similar. This accounted for the short length of service to Faresaver that some Mercs gave.

WESTERN GREYHOUND LTD, NEWQUAY.
This company was set up in 1998 by two former FirstBus senior managers, Mark Howarth and Robin Orbell, who were seeking new opportunities in the bus industry. Mark had come from the local First Western National operation, so was very familiar with Cornwall's needs. The desire to enter Cornish operations was timely, as three local small businesses were looking to sell up.

Western Greyhound therefore took over their school contracts and some coaches. At the end of the first year, though, Western Greyhound won the contracts from Cornwall Council for two regular bus services. These, the 592 and 594, linked Truro with Newquay or Wadebridge. For the services, Western Greyhound placed an order for three new midibuses but, so as to be ready to take up the contracts, three Mercs were hired. Eurotaxis of Bristol lent them Mellor B27F-bodied 709D M675 TNA, while dealer Simon Munden, also of Bristol, lent two of the early, ground-breaking, van-conversion 709Ds that had been new to Newcastle Busways, then with Devon General, D408/13 TFT. In January 1999, though, the three new buses were placed in service. These were Mercedes-Benz Varios, with Plaxton Beaver 2 DP27F bodywork. They were registered locally as S501-3 SRL.

The first new Merc delivered to Western Greyhound was S501 SRL, a Vario with Plaxton Beaver 2 bodywork, seating 27. It is seen in Wadebridge on one of the company's two original contracted services.

Further regular work followed, as First Western National was putting less emphasis on the western and northern parts of Cornwall. Western Greyhound began to expand rapidly through contract wins and, by working to clock-face timetables and with catchy publicity, its services became well-known and well-used. Their buses became familiar to visitors, too, as they served picturesque Cornish fishing villages and sandy bays, or remote country villages, nearly all reached by narrow lanes. Before very long, the company was serving most parts of Cornwall and they even reached Exeter in Devon, to give a spread of nearly 120 miles to their territory.

Although coaches and double-deckers also featured in the fleet, the Mercedes-Benz midibus formed the backbone of the stock. Unusually, though, only a few were T2s. A 709D with Reeve-Burgess Beaver DP25F body, E301 BWL, new to Thames Transit in Oxford, came not long after operations began, but the only other T2 to enter service arrived eighteen months later. It was an 811D with Beaver B33F bodywork, G896 TGG. Previously with Arriva East Herts & Essex, this one was immediately re-registered UWR 498.

The arrival of the three new Mercedes-Benz Varios started a standardisation on that model and no more T2s were acquired. Standardisation even extended to the bodywork, as all Varios carried Plaxton Beaver 2 bodies and, with few exceptions, they were equipped with 33 coach seats.

New Varios from late 2001, which were registered in the new system, again had local marks, but always with the distinctive local identifier of WK ('West-country, Kernow',

THE MERCEDES-BENZ MIDIBUS IN SOUTH WEST ENGLAND • 159

The T2 version of the Mercedes-Benz turned out to be a rarity in the Western Greyhound fleet. The second yet final example to be owned was this 811D-Reeve-Burgess Beaver 33-seater. New as G896 TGG, it was soon re-registered with 'dateless' mark UWR 498. It is seen in Henver Road, Newquay.

Kernow, of course, being the name of the county in the Cornish language). Earlier Varios bought second-hand were often re-registered with the appropriate year prefix-letter, then a distinctive two-digit number and, finally, the letters WGL, representing the company's initials (although, by coincidence, WGL had latterly been a Truro issue). Second-hand Varios new since 2001 were re-registered with WK numberplates for the appropriate half-year. Some had humorous marks, such as WK03 DAD, or WK56 SUN and SET.

Western Greyhound initially painted their buses in an eye-catching livery of pink and white. With the increasing use by First Western National of the 'Barbie' liveries, which included magenta relief, Western Greyhound changed their scheme to bright-green and white.

In later years, Western Greyhound began to choose the Optare Solo for fleet additions, but the Vario fleet reached a remarkable peak of sixty-two examples.

During the early hours of 13 May 2013, a fire engulfed the Summercourt depot. Despite the efforts of the Fire Brigade, thirty-four buses were destroyed (about one third of the fleet). Loans appeared from operators far and wide. Some scorched buses were able to be repaired, while some withdrawn buses were re-activated, most of these receiving a repaint into all-over green. The effects of the fire could have been much worse had many of the buses – mainly Varios – not been parked overnight at numerous rural outstations. Forensics showed the fire to have been started by arsonists.

Above: Western Greyhound later changed their colour-scheme, as shown by this scene outside Newquay bus-station. Representing the outgoing pink and white is ex-James (Andybus) of Tetbury R810 HWS, while in the new green and white is X33 WGL (formerly X437 JHS with Wilson of Rhu).

Below: Cornwall has a number of beautiful beaches and many are excellent for surfing. In this picture, a lot of people can be seen in the water. Many of the coves are only reached by steep, twisty hills, which the Western Greyhound Varios took in their stride. Here, WK02 SAT climbs out of Polzeath, southbound for Wadebridge. The bus was new as SK02 NZB with Fairline of Glasgow.

Above: Down by the crowded beach at Polzeath, heading north to Camelford, is W349 WCS, acquired from Rowe of Kilmarnock.

Below: This Vario had always been in Cornwall, but not with Western Greyhound all of the time. It began life with Hambly of Pelynt, on cherished Cornish registration WAF 156. It was re-registered WK04 HSD when passing to Western Greyhound, at two years of age. It is seen in West Looe.

Following the devastating arson attack on the Summercourt depot in 2013, some scorched Varios, being prepared for returning to service, were repainted all-over green. Included was WK51 HNF, one of the buses delivered new to the company. It is seen in Boscastle.

The fire, and another at the Liskeard parking area less than a year later, had a major effect on finances, compounded by complications over insurance pay-outs. The reduction of the government's concessionary fare re-imbursement scheme was already having a marked effect and the end result was that Western Greyhound became unsustainable. In March 2015, the company ceased trading.

ACL TRAVEL, WESTON-SUPER-MARE

This is a tale of ambition, determination and competition, but also of sudden collapse. It ably demonstrates the precarious nature of work in the bus industry, particularly since Deregulation.

Messrs Bowden and Jones started trading in 2006, with two coaches and two minibuses. They next bought a 14-year-old Mercedes-Benz 811D/Plaxton Beaver coach. This was soon re-registered from K922 UFX to RLZ 7361. Early the next year, when North Somerset Council invited tenders for two Weston-super-Mare town services, it was ACL Travel who submitted the winning bids. The contracts were for the 83, between Worlebury, the town centre and Bleadon, and the 85, from the town centre to St Georges. The routes were taken up on 1 April 2007, for which ACL had obtained a pair of Stagecoach-standard Mercedes-Benz 709D/Alexander Sprint 25-seaters, M653/4 FYS. They came from Stagecoach Western Scottish and, for a while, they remained in latest Stagecoach livery, but with large ACL Travel fleetnames.

THE MERCEDES-BENZ MIDIBUS IN SOUTH WEST ENGLAND • 163

Stagecoach livery in the heart of Badgerline territory, in Weston-super-Mare. But the large fleetnames, of ACL Travel, dispel the myth. M653 FYS is one of two ex-Stagecoach Western Scottish 709Ds, with Alexander Sprint bodies, that ACL Travel obtained to start their contracted services.

During the May Day Bank-Holiday weekend, M654 FYS was repainted to show off ACL Travel's bright new image – a livery of all-over orange. Fleet-numbers were now being applied and these became 9 and 10, the 811D coach being numbered 5.

Following the purchase of a full-sized Dennis Lance (12) for a service to Bristol, another Stagecoach-standard 709D/Alexander Sprint was acquired in the June and outshopped in orange (13). This was N943 NAP, from Stagecoach East Kent. It had been obtained for ACL Travel's first service aimed at competing against the incumbent First Somerset & Avon, on Weston-super-Mare town routes. It was activated early, in fact, to enable M653 FYS to be painted out of Stagecoach colours.

The new service commenced on 2 July, to duplicate First Somerset & Avon's busy route 7 to Worle, via Milton Road, but from the town centre only. ACL called their service the 06. At the end of November, however – on a Friday, strangely – the 06 was extended across town, to duplicate the 7 all the way to/from Oldmixon. Obtained for the extra commitments was a rather different Merc. Although again from a Stagecoach fleet, former Stagecoach Devon R102 NTA was a Vario, with Alexander ALX100 body. It was numbered 14. Meanwhile, in the September, the 811D/Beaver coach had been repainted into the orange and now appeared quite regularly on bus services in the town.

In February 2008, ACL obtained number 15, the first of several Dennis Darts or, later, Volvo B6s, mainly with Alexander Dash bodywork – and still coming from Stagecoach fleets. All was not lost for the Merc T2, though, and a need for

ACL Travel's third ex-Stagecoach Alexander-bodied Merc was rather different, as it was a Vario with ALX100 bodywork. R102 NTA was previously Stagecoach Devon 102.

extra stock was met with the hiring of 709Ds, with Plaxton Beaver bodies, from NextBus of Chippenham, this being the sales division of Faresaver, whose white and lilac livery was carried.

In April, for a route competing with First's 5 and numbered 05 (Uphill-town centre-Upper Bristol Road-Worle), three more Alexander Sprint 709Ds appeared in service, numbered 16 to 18. Although new to, or intended for, Stagecoach Bluebird Buses of Aberdeen, these had again run for Stagecoach Western Scottish for some time and were N639, 610 & 638 VSS.

At the end of the year, ACL started working on route 01, duplicating First's 1 from the town centre, then north along the promenade, past the piers, along the coast and out to Sand Bay and its holiday centres which, even in winter, have a faithful clientele, but enough custom for two operators? Probably not, although at certain times of the day each company's bus was seen to take on a good load, even filling up a 709D. Meanwhile, the existing routes were being tweaked when possible, to improve the level of service.

ACL started 2009 with another competing route, the 02. This followed First's 13 to Uphill, via Whitecross Road, and was seen to be worked by any bus. Later, ACL won another council contract. This was for a new service, the 16, via Locking Castle and a great deal of new housing, to West Wick, commencing in April 2009. This was part-funded by the developers and was worked by a Merc.

It appeared that First Somerset & Avon was feeling the effects of the relentless competition because, in May 2009, they implemented considerable retrenchment in the town and

Above: In April 2008, three more 709D-Sprints were added, including N639 VSS, again from Stagecoach Western Scottish. It is working on the 06, designed to compete with First's service 7.

Below: In January 2008, another operator had started competing on Weston-super-Mare town services. This was termed 'In One Spin Travel', run by Steve Minor, and worked a route 2, to Bourneville Estate. A variety of single-deckers and even a double-decker appeared, short term and in a variety of colours. There were also two Mercs. Seen here is longer-lasting N574 CEH. Remarkably, this bus had worked in Weston before – as First Bristol 3974. It was one of those that came from First PMT in 2001, as described above. The other Merc was an all-white 33-seat 811D, L662 CYG. In One Spin ceased running in the July.

simplified the remaining network, which put several of their 709Ds out of work. The contract that First held for service 4, a hilly and difficult circular route serving the older part of the town, was surrendered, but re-issued to ACL Travel (from the town centre only, but still needing two 709Ds). This must have boosted ACL's confidence. Furthermore, as First's Mercedes-operated route 3 was being simplified, the Council diverted ACL's contracted route 85 in part-compensation. Yet another Stagecoach 709D-Sprint was now placed in service, N215 UHH coming from Stagecoach in Cumbria. This took the fleet-numbering to 28.

Despite all that, on Sunday, 16 August 2009 and with no warning, ACL Travel ceased to trade and all staff were dismissed. On the Monday morning, there was no service on the contracted routes 04, 16, 83 or 85. North Somerset Council was in frantic action as soon as the news broke, trying to arrange with other operators to cover these supported services. The sudden collapse of ACL Travel illustrates the level of inconvenience placed not only on the employees, but on the travelling public, the council staff and other bus providers. On the other hand, First Somerset & Avon was pleased to be back to running alone on the routes that ACL had duplicated. They never reinstated the withdrawn routes, however.

Happily, agreement was reached quickly for replacement operators to take on the four funded routes and emergency contracts were issued, though it is believed that it took until the Wednesday before everything was in place. First took back the 4 (on an hourly headway only, so requiring just one bus – a 709D) and also took on the 16. Ironically, they needed to draft in an extra Merc 709D to cover. The incoming bus came up from Taunton, but was originally a Bristol City Line bus, formerly 7902 (N902 HWS) and now numbered 51602. It made route 4 its own. A second Merc was brought up by the next week

With the sudden collapse of ACL Travel, North Somerset Council had to act quickly to obtain cover for the four contracted routes. The 83 and 85 were awarded to Coombs Travel. Their 29-seat 709D with Dormobile Routemaker 2 coachwork, K721 HYA, is seen here, on the 83.

and this was very interesting in being a Vario, with Beaver 2 bodywork, not a type familiar in the local First fleet. Numbered 52532 (S532 RWP), it was one of a large fleet that had been new to Midland Red West. Originally, only 22 seats had been installed, though it now had seating for 27. Many of the batch had latterly run for First Devon & Cornwall and indeed this one came from Barnstaple. Its new home was on route 16.

Routes 83 and 85 were both accepted by a local coach operator, Coombs Travel. Coombs happened to have four Mercedes-Benz midis of their own, all bought new and with coach-type seats, but suitable for stage work on the contracted rural services that they already ran. Three were Varios, comprising an Optare Nouvelle 2 (W371 PHY) and two Beaver 2s (WP52 WHG and WU03 FJY). The fourth Merc was now 17 years old, but perfectly presentable. K721 HYA was a 709D, with Dormobile Routemaker 2 DP29F coachwork. Any two of these could work the two duties.

North Somerset Council then drew up new contracts, the first one to start on 7 September. The successful winner of the tender for the 4 this time round was the largest of the town's coach operators, Bakers Dolphin (JN Baker Ltd.). Among over 100 vehicles, Bakers had a 709D with Plaxton Beaver long tailed B27F bodywork. It was new as N194 EMJ with Luton & District, though it had recently been re-registered UKZ 5491. As the 4 was being restored to its full length across to Hutton, at a half-hourly frequency, Bakers decided to hire a Merc while they sought a bus to buy. This came from David Hoare's Chepstow Classic Bus fleet and was painted all-over blue. It was of a type now well known in the town – a Stagecoach-standard Alexander Sprint 709D. In fact, it was new to Stagecoach West, in the Cheltenham District Traction Company division,

Having won the new contract for the 4, in place of ACL Travel, Bakers Dolphin was able to use their ex-Arriva East Herts & Essex Plaxton Beaver-709D, UKZ 5491 (ex-N194 EMJ). Neatly printed paper destination displays are one thing, but are of limited benefit when laid on a Merc's dash.

Hired to Bakers later was this Merc of a familiar outline for the town – an ex-Stagecoach Alexander Sprint-709D. N730 RDD was new to Cheltenham & Gloucester, but was now owned by David Hoare's Chepstow Classic Bus.

and was N730 RDD. Displaced now from the 4, First's 51602 was found other work in the town, usually on the 3.

A week later, the new contract for the 16 also became Bakers' responsibility and more Mercs were hired. These were in Faresaver colours and came from NextBus of Chippenham who, of course, had supplied similar buses to ACL Travel early the previous year. The buses hired to Bakers, though, were Beaver 2-bodied Varios, so such buses, never common in the area, were currently being run on town services by three operators. The white-and-lilac NextBus Varios were R117 TKO and W806 PKS. First's Vario, 52532, displaced from the 16, was found other work locally. David Hoare exchanged the Alexander Sprint 709D that he was hiring to Bakers for N716 KAM, which had been new to Stagecoach West's Swindon & District division.

Also from 14 September, North Somerset Council's contract for the 85, which was being run by Coombs, was cancelled, passengers being invited to *walk* to their nearest First bus-stop.

From the end of October, Bakers started placing into service (after a repaint into their light-blue and white livery) second-hand Optare Solos. With First Somerset & Avon also transferring some Optare Solos to Weston, plus some Dennis Dart SLFs, November 2009 saw the withdrawal of the last of all their Mercedes-Benz 709Ds here – bar one bus. 51107 (L907 VHT) remained in service just into the first week of December 2009. This marked the end of no less than 18 years of operation of Mercedes-Benz 709D-Beavers in the town, since Badgerline days. The L-VHTs, new to Bath of course, had themselves given a very creditable 15 years. It should be noted, though, that First still had five Merc T2s in the town, but these were ex-First Southern National 811Ds, with Wright Nimbus bodies. The drafted-in Vario, 52532, was also still active as was Bakers' 709D, which was making fairly frequent appearances on the 4.

THE MERCEDES-BENZ MIDIBUS IN SOUTH WEST ENGLAND • 169

Even these new contracts were only valid until the end of the original term as issued to ACL Travel, which was until April 2010. On re-tendering, the 4, 16, 83 and a reinstated 85 were all awarded to a newcomer to the town's services, Webberbus of Bridgwater. Webberbus had already been competing with First on the service between the two towns and was subsequently to start competing on Weston town services – a touch of déjà vu, there. Webberbus ordered a fleet of new Optare Solo SRs for their gained routes.

First's Wright-bodied 811Ds were themselves withdrawn from Weston-super-Mare during this same year, 2010 and, late in the year, Vario 52532 was transferred down to Taunton.

THE ST IVES PARK & RIDE – 4, 3, 2, 1.

The Park & Ride service operated at the popular Cornish tourist resort of St Ives during one particular summer was notable and it appears to have been a unique operation. The summer was that of 2007, when the service, between a large carpark high above the town and the narrow streets of the town centre, was run by *four* Mercedes-Benz T2s, of *three* clearly different types, owned by *two* operators, running this *one* service.

The St Ives Bus Company Ltd owned two of the buses in use. L226 JFA was a 709D, with Dormobile Routemaker 2 B29F body. It was new in 1993 to Stevensons of Spath. Their second bus was L858 COD, an 811D with Marshall C16 B33F body. This was new in 1994 to Dart Line (Dealtop) of Exeter.

The other two buses were owned by N Eastwood of St Ives and made a matching pair. The buses were further 811Ds, but these two carried Alexander (Belfast) B31F bodywork. They were N718/9 DJC and were new in 1995 to the Arriva Cymru fleet.

With St Ives' sandy harbour and the tower of the Parish Church visible a long way below, Dormobile Routemaker 2-bodied 709D L226 JFA awaits custom at the town's main car-park. The bus is owned by the St Ives Bus Company.

In contrast, the St Ives Bus Company's other Park & Ride bus was L858 COD, an 811D with Marshall bodywork. Behind it is one of a pair of Alexander Sprint 811Ds, run on the same service by N. Eastwood of St Ives.

FIRSTBUS

THE NATIONAL FLEET RE-NUMBERING SCHEME OF JANUARY 2004: AN OUTLINE OF THE RENUMBERING OF MERCEDES MIDIBUSES IN SOUTH-WEST ENGLAND

In 2002, FirstBus decided to adopt a single numbering system for its entire stock of buses and coaches, wherever they may be in the country. Because of the vast quantity of buses involved, the new numbers comprised five digits. These were stated to be 'numbers for life', so would never need to be changed, even if a vehicle was transferred to a different FirstBus subsidiary. This was no disadvantage.

The initial phase of renumbering was implemented from the summer of 2002, starting with Potteries Motor Traction in the north Midlands, before continuing to Northern England and Scotland. However, other than the use of a common initial numeral to denote the category of bus – numbers beginning at 30000, for example, were double-deckers, while 50000 upwards was reserved for midibuses – the allocation of the new numbers was totally shambolic. It took no regard of the make of the bus, or even whether it had a step at the entrance doorway or was a low-floor, fully-accessible model; batches of such buses were often intermixed. The new number bore no relation to either the original fleet-number, nor the registration number, despite many operators going to great lengths to ensure that both items matched, for the benefit of operations staff. As an example, a batch of Merc 709Ds with Beaver bodies new to PMT as 420-429 (P420-429 MEH) were now numbered 50077/8, 50164-9 and 50079/80, merely because P422-7 MEH had been moved to Greater Manchester, so were dealt with later. A vehicle's age was not considered – earlier 709Ds still with PMT had higher numbers than these, while many PMT Varios had lower numbers than the P-MEHs. The M-VWU batch of 709D-Beavers new to West Yorkshire was now so scattered that their new numbers ranged between 50130 and 50422. The worst case, probably, was in Aberdeen where First had its headquarters. 50411-50427 were allocated randomly to eight different types on Merc.

Before the renumbering affected the fleets in the East and West Midlands, South Wales and the South of England (which, importantly, included

THE MERCEDES-BENZ MIDIBUS

the rather particular London fleets), there had been a major re-think and an orderly system was devised.

Midibuses in the north (where Iveco 49-10s and Optare Solos were intermingled with the Mercs) had taken the new numbers up towards 50500. In the south, Mercedes-Benz midibuses alone were given numbers above that (with a few specific exceptions, mentioned below), while the other makes were placed into separate sub-series. This time, the numbers were carefully allocated. As far as possible, they were in age order and – helpfully – they generally matched the numbers in their registrations even when the operators, such as Southern National, had not bothered to match originally. What the new system did not do was to differentiate between shorter and longer Mercs, therefore disregarding the segregations chosen by Southern National and Western National.

Below is a list of the relevant renumbering. It should be borne in mind that, by this time, a number of Mercs had either been withdrawn or transferred out of the area. It will be noticed that six elderly Mercs were given un-matched numbers at the end of the 50400s – these were 'odd men out' by this time and due for early withdrawal. With such a large number of Mercs hopefully being allocated near-matching new numbers, it is understandable that, in a few cases, it was not possible to match. An example of this is shown early in the list below, where two buses had registrations that happened to start with J610.

NOTE – In the following list, the symbol # indicates an incomplete batch, either because withdrawals and transfers had taken place, or because certain numbers had been left out due to suitable registration numbers being unobtainable in the first place. Other footnotes are explained at the end of the list. The abbreviations used for the operators in the south-west are as follows:

Btl = First Bristol; H&D = First Hampshire & Dorset; S&A = First Somerset & Avon; W.N. = First Western National.			
50486	E694 UND	S&A 3912	609D / Made-to-Measure van conv.
50488	E812 MOU	W.N. 6329	811D / Optare StarRider
50490	F154 RHK	H&D 774	811D / Reeve-Burgess
50491	F949 BMS	W.N. 6284	811D / Alexander
50492	G152 GOL	W.N. 6302	811D / Carlyle
50493	F652 XMS	W.N. 6290	811D / Alexander
50624	H324 HVT	W.N. 6500	609D / PMT (ex-Plymouth Argyle FC)
50703/4/6	H893/4/6 LOX	W.N. 6308/9/11	811D / Carlyle
50710	J610 HMF	Red Bus 6387	811D / Reeve Burgess
50711	J610 PTA	Red Bus 6370	811D / Carlyle-Marshall
50718/726	H718/26 HGL	W.N. 6318/26	811D / Carlyle
50740-6/8	J140-6/8 SJT	Red Bus 6520-4/6-8	709D / Wright
50757/8	J857/8 FTC	S&A 3857/8	709D / Reeve Burgess
50829	K29 OEU	S&A 3916	709D / Wright

50831-843	K331-343 OAF	W.N. 6331-6343	811D/Plaxton
50844-854	K344-354 ORL	W.N. 6344-6354	811D/Plaxton
50870/1	K434/441 XRF	S&A 3934/41	709D/Plaxton
50901-923#	K601-623 ORL	W.N. 6601-6623	709D/Plaxton
50950	K723 WTT	Red Bus 6529	709D/Wright
50952-955	K752-755 XTA	Red Bus 6371-4	811D/Wright
50967-976#	K867-876 NEU	S&A 3867-76	709D/Plaxton
50990-994#	K690-694 UFV	S&A 8311-5	709D/Plaxton
51001-026#	L801-826 SAE	Btl and S&A 7801-7826 (i)	709D/Plaxton
51029	L829 WHY	Btl 7829	709D/Plaxton
51077	L877 TFB	S&A 3877	711D/Plaxton
51078-51111#	L878-911 VHT	S&A 3878-3911	709D/Plaxton
51129/130	L329/330 MYC	S&A 759, H&D 760	811D/Wright
51141-151#	L641-651 VCV	W.N. 6641-6651	709D/Plaxton
51155-160	L355-360 VCV	W.N. 6355-6360	811D/Plaxton
51167-169	L67-9 EPR	S&A 761/2, Red Bus 6375	811D/Wright
51192	L92 NSF	S&A 749	709D/Alexander
51210-212	L650-652 CJT	H&D 756, S&A 757/8	811D/Wright
51214/9	M14, 19 ABC	S&A 747/8	709D/Alexander
51220	M220 PMS	H&D 736	709D/Alexander
51226	M226 VWU	W.N. (now Red Bus) 6653	709D/Plaxton
51239/240	M239/40 VYA	H&D 734/5	709D/Alexander
51241/243	M241/2 VYA	S&A 770/1	811D/Wright
51246	M246 VWU	W.N. (now Red Bus) 6652	709D/Plaxton
51278/9/81/2	M278/9/81/2 UYD	H&D 730-733	709D/Alexander
51305	M305 TSF	S&A 725	709D/Alexander
51308/309	M508/509 VYA	S&A 772, H&D 773	811D/Wright
51345/6/8	M45/6/8 BEG	S&A 8307/8/10	811D/Marshall
51370	M968 USC	S&A 8306	814D/Plaxton
51372/373	M372/373 XEX	S&A 650/1	609D/Frank Guy van con'vn.
51374-378	M674-678 RAJ	S&A 953/4, Red Bus 6533-5	709D/Alexander
51380	M882 BEU	S&A 3882	709D/Plaxton
51381-382	M381/2 KVR	S&A 958/9	709D/Alexander
51385/8/9	M765/8/9 FTT	Red Bus 6377/9/80	811D/Marshall
51390/1	M764/6 FTT	Red Bus 6376, H&D 766	811D/Marshall
51386/392/3	M386/92/3 KVR	S&A 952/0/1	709D/Alexander
51401/402	M901/2 LTT	W.N. 6531/2	609D/Frank Guy van con'vn

51403-405	M803-5 UYA	S&A 727/6/8	709D/Alexander
51531-574#	M831-874 ATC	Btl and S&A 7831-7874 (ii)	709D/Plaxton
51556	M857 XHY	S&A 8309	811D/Marshall (iii)
51575-607#	N875-907 HWS	S&A and H&D 7875-7907	709D/Plaxton
51609-11/3/22/3	N609/5/11/3/22/3 GAH	S&A 653/2/4-7	609D/Frank Guy van con'vn
51646	N46 OAE	H&D 737	709D/Alexander (iv)
51656-9/661	N556-9/561 EYB	H&D 738 and S&A 739-742	709D/Alexander
51679/80/2/3	P179/80/2/3 LYB	S&A 786/7/9/90	711D/Plaxton
51684-6/8	N584/3/6/8 WND	S&A 969/71/70/68	709D/Alexander
51719	N719 GRV	W.N. 6659	709DPlaxton
51742/3/5-8	P442/3/5-8 KYC	S&A 780-785	711D/Alexander
51880	P181 LYB	S&A 788	711D/Plaxton (v)

The Mercedes-Benz Varios, being fewer in quantity, were easier to match to new numbers:

52565-572	S865-872 NOD	Red Bus 6704-6711
52573/574	S863/864 LRU	S&A 863/4 (vi)
52601-608	R501-508 NPR	H&D 854-861
52640	S340 WYB	S&A 862
52650	R650 TDV	Red Bus 6700
52651	R851 YDV	Red Bus 6701
52652/653	R852/853 TFJ	Red Bus 6702/3

NOTES:

(i) L809 SAE was currently Western National 6675.
(ii) M844/50/60/70 ATC were currently Western National 6681-4.
(iii) There was no real reason why M857 XHY should not have stayed with the rest of its batch, as 51347, rather than 51556. At least, it would then have been a better match.
(iv) 51646 had been re-registered N46 OAE from TDZ 3265 in 3/01, while Southern National was under the wing of First Bristol.
(v) The reason for numbering P181 LYB as 51880, rather than 51681, has not been discovered. (The number 51881 was allocated to First Eastern Counties P681 HND – so not even that bus was allocated 51681)
(vi) The numbers 52563/4 were allocated, correctly, to the last of the Midland Red West sequence of 64 Varios, S563/4 RWP.

SCALE MODEL MERCEDES-BENZ MIDIBUSES

For many years, railway modellers who have built realistic OO-scale railway layouts have tried to add road vehicles in the same scale, which interprets as 1/76th size. The vehicles often had to be made from kits. Models of buses were normally only found among those made as toys, however realistic. At the end of the 1980s, however, Exclusive First Editions, or EFE, came on to the market, starting with a 1/76th scale model of the popular London RT double-decker. The idea became enormously popular with bus enthusiasts and EFE's range of buses expanded rapidly.

In time, EFE turned to modelling a midibus. Their choice was the most popular of all the real-life options, the short wheelbase Mercedes-Benz T2, with Reeve-Burgess or Plaxton Beaver bodywork. The outcome was very realistic. It was soon marketed in a wide range of authentic liveries, complete with fleet-numbers and registration plates. Furthermore, a version with the original shallow destination box was also produced.

Subsequently, a rival range of 1/76th models was launched, under the banner of the Original Omnibus Company, or OOC. This company soon introduced a midibus as well. In this case, the choice fell on the Mercedes-Benz Vario, with Plaxton Beaver 2 bodywork. It, too, appeared in a range of authentic liveries.

Since the late-eighties, the production of accurate scale-model buses has been big business. The Mercedes-Benz midibus was modelled by two of the main concerns, in a range of authentic liveries. On the right in this photograph are two Beaver-bodied 709Ds produced by EFE, one appearing as First Eastern Counties 875 (H354 LJN, the real bus having been transferred from Thamesway), the other being an early example with the shallow destination box, Brewers of Maesteg 428 (E288 VEP, transferred from parent South Wales Transport and later moved to Western National). On the left of the picture is OOC's offering, a Beaver 2-bodied Vario, this example being First Eastern National 2703 (P703 PWC).